"There are still a few—maybe only two—generations of people in parts of North America who might recognize some of the history which anchors this memoir; the Civil rights movement in the United States, the anti-war efforts of the 1960s led by students, the international liberation movements, the names of famous Black leaders. (...) *Eyes Have Seen* grants necessary access to how ordinary people living full lives—as children, parents, grandparents, farmers, churchgoers, educators, friends, artists, lovers, sisters, and brothers—become compelled to respond to acts and systems harmful to the fulfilment of their humanity, which result in extraordinary actions for the greater good of so many more who will be the unknowing beneficiaries of their sacrifices." — **Nantali Indongo, Host-Producer of CBC's *The Bridge***

"The captivating story of Fred Anderson, aka Clifford Gaston, is rooted in the African-American traditions of the American South. (...) Fred Anderson's life has been shaped by the great moments of North American history, from the African-American civil rights movement and the mobilization against the Vietnam war to, on our side of the border, the Montreal Congress of Black Writers, the Sir George Williams affair, and the October Crisis of 1970. *Eyes Have Seen* is a fascinating read that leaves you awed and inspired." — **Aly Ndiaye, aka Webster**

"A masterpiece. *Eyes Have Seen* is brilliant, erudite storytelling in well-limned, lyrical and cinematic prose. These days, as the USA endeavours to lie about its white supremacist legacy, this memoir is a searing reminder of Jim Crow and its cost: in lives, in property, its psychological terror, and the exile suffered by those who endured or fought it. The latter half of the memoir, which depicts Anderson's life as a Vietnam-War draft resister in Montreal, is an invaluable contribution to history." — **Nigel Thomas, author of *A Different Hurricane***

"Fred Anderson's story is a gripping tale that maps the terrain of Black family and exile at a moment of a certain Black becoming. The Civil Rights Movement and Black Power continue to reverberate for all of us and Anderson's intimate account of his experience through the movement and exile to Canada is not just one of triumph but a reckoning with a past that is not yet behind us. (...) Read this memoir and sit with its many truths and its difficult triumphs!" — **Rinaldo Walcott,** Professor, Africana and American Studies, University of Buffalo.

"Congratulations, Fred Anderson, one of the bravest men I have ever known. He was a favorite of Ms Ella Gaston @Justice for Ella for his courage against the deadly odds of the 1960s Civil Rights fight in Mississippi." — **Pam Johnson, author of Justice for Ella, A Story that Needed to be Told.**

# EYES HAVE SEEN

FRED ANDERSON

# EYES HAVE SEEN

## From Mississippi to Montreal

A Memoir

Baraka
Books
Montréal

All rights reserved. No part of this book may be reproduced or transmitted in any form or by any means, electronic or mechanical, including photocopying, recording, or by any information storage and retrieval system, without permission in writing from the publisher.

© 2025 Fred Anderson
ISBN 978-1-77186-378-0 pbk; 978-1-77186-387-2 epub;
978-1-77186-388-9 pdf

Cover by Leila Marshy
Book Design by Folio infographie
Editing: Robin Philpot
Proofreading: Anne Marie Marko, Rachel Hewitt

Legal Deposit, 2nd quarter 2025
Bibliothèque et Archives nationales du Québec
Library and Archives Canada

Published by Baraka Books of Montreal

Printed and bound in Quebec

TRADE DISTRIBUTION & RETURNS

Canada
UTPdistribution.com

United States
Independent Publishers Group: IPGbook.com

We acknowledge the support from the Société de développement des entreprises culturelles (SODEC) and the Government of Quebec tax credit for book publishing administered by SODEC.

# CONTENTS

INTRODUCTION
**Aperture** 1
Whose Story Is it Anyway? 4
Lord, it's a Miracle 5

## PART I

CHAPTER ONE
**Beginnings**  9
**The Hub City**
Maggie 12
A Childhood Harvest 18
Keeper of Tales, Mistress of Poultices 20
Storm Clouds Gather 24
If Mobile Street Could Talk 26
ABCs of Race 28
As Quick as You Can Say Jackie Robinson 30
Tambourines to Glory 32
I Got Wings 37

CHAPTER TWO
**A Band of Brothers and Sisters** 39
**Circle of Trust**
A Fly in the Buttermilk 44
Belly of the Whale 47
Fortuity 49
The Chosen Few 53

CHAPTER THREE
**Greenville, Mississippi** 55
**Queen of the Mississippi Delta**
Antebellum Blues 58
Out on a Limb 59
Ballots or Bullets 63
Unlock Me, Lord 64
If Not Action, Then Intent 66
On the Road from Damascus 67

# PART II

CHAPTER FOUR
**Mississippi Freedom Summer** 75
Asking the Right Questions 76
Uncommon Knowledge 79
Driving While Black 81
Standing in the Need of Prayer, Lord 85
A Storm A'Brewin' 90
"Ninety-nine and a half miles won't do." 93
Euphemisms Kill 96
Baptism 99
The Pen and the Sword 100
Ghosting 102
A Lasting Sense of Grievance 103
Grifting 105

CHAPTER FIVE
**Gone Already** 109
Flash Flood 110
The Albany Movement 112
Let Us Prey 114
Which Way, Lord 116
Dreaming Freedom 117

CHAPTER SIX
**Swing Low, Sweet Chariot** 121
Harlem of the North 123
Paris of North America 131

CHAPTER SEVEN
**Mariners All** 135

CHAPTER EIGHT
**Day of Cargo** 143

CHAPTER NINE
**Gonna Be a Long Night** 151
Noel Noir 157

CHAPTER TEN
**All That Jazz and a Convergence of Political Consciousness** 161
Masquerades 170

# PART III

CHAPTER ELEVEN
**Abeyance** 177
Home Comes to Montreal 178
Some Stars Shine Less Brightly 181
Unwilled 182

CHAPTER TWELVE
**Snow of a Different Kind** 185

CHAPTER THIRTEEN
**State of Apprehended Insurrection** 191
Medicinal 194
Stories Don't Tell Themselves 198

CHAPTER FOURTEEN
**A Blues for Clifford** 203

CHAPTER FIFTEEN
**A Dream Deferred** 213
My Kingdom for an Ark 217
Take Me to the Water 229
Above the Tree Line 230

**EPILOGUE** 237
September 24, 2021 237

**ACKNOWLEDGEMENTS**
Homage 239
In Memoriam 239

*Dedicated to Damon Thomas Anderson*

"We were navigating our rafts in the rapids of history's currents and couldn't quite imagine how 'things come together'... Dorie and Joyce Ladner, Mattie Bivens, and Fred Anderson from Hattiesburg... Thirty-plus Black high school graduates and Black college students came together in that pressured space-time to work 24/7, to get knocked down and get back up..."

—*Constitutional People: Written Testimony of Robert P. Moses*, submitted to The United States Senate Judiciary Committee, Tuesday, September 4, 2007.

INTRODUCTION
# APERTURE

*"Memory knows before knowing remembers"*
—William Faulkner, *Light in August* (1932)

I have attempted many beginnings at this memoir, but floundered amidst the many personal losses of family, friends, SNCC veterans, and my political exile in Canada. It is the inevitability of the encroaching metronomic hour. The insistent urgency of making meanings, the exegesis of time, and the weight of receding memory that brings me back to the blank pages of necessity.

I was fifteen when I left home, sucked into the maelstrom of the U.S. southern civil rights movement. It was an exhilarating and dangerous life working as a field secretary for the Student Non-Violent Coordinating Committee (SNCC)—riding the tides of ascendancy and decline of, arguably, the most preeminent organization of the movement for civil rights. SNCC was in decline in the late summer of 1965. Our policies against the Vietnam War and the support of liberation movements in Africa and other Third World countries were considered controversial. Some white liberals and Jewish donors were particularly outraged with our advocacy for nationhood for Palestine. The U.S. State Department was equally chagrined with our championing the divestment campaign against the apartheid regime of South Africa. Our actions were targeted by the Federal Bureau of Investigation (FBI). A campaign of disinformation, entrapment, and assassinations ensued. The military draft boards systemically and disproportionately inducted social activists, poor blacks, and white allied activists—a supply line for the Indo-China War and decimation of the ranks of SNCC.

SNCC staffers, on November 6 through 12, 1964, retreated to Gulfside Methodist Church in Waveland, Mississippi. We gathered to evaluate the state of the organization—to explore and pursue alternative funding sources. We were a battle-scarred and weary band of brothers and sisters. We had little understanding of how much each of us was psychologically and emotionally frayed. The notion of "post-traumatic stress disorder" was yet unnamed and mostly unrecognized. The assembly reviewed thirty-seven anonymously submitted position papers: examining goals, ideology, organizing tactics, decision-making schema, race, and gender relations among staff. The goal of unauthored submissions was to ensure, regardless of hierarchical demarcations, that no one voice, or philosophical or political stance would unduly outweigh others in the decision-making process. This approach was foundational to SNCC's ethos of participatory democracy. However, we were all too familiar with each other's writing, theoretical underpinnings, and self-presentation styles. Heated debate ensued and led to bitter dispute and recriminations. One anonymously submitted document critically examining the problem of sexism in the organization was mercurial and divisive. The rigorous discussions lasted for hours long after day had turned to night.

The opening session ended with the election of executive officers. John Lewis was reconfirmed as SNCC chairman. Most of us wearily retired to our cabins. A call went out for all to return to the main hall. Yawning, bleary-eyed, we reassembled. It was announced that a long-term SNCC veteran had contested the election outcome. A recount elevated Stokely Carmichael over John Lewis. Lewis was visibly shaken and personally wounded. Many agreed it had been a coup d'etat.

The Waveland Retreat represented a cataclysmic juncture for SNCC and the civil rights movement. The fissures and failure to broker consent accelerated a downward trajectory over the next several years. The Waveland Retreat was followed by conferences in Atlanta, Georgia, in February 1965, and the infamous Peg Leg Bates Estate summit in upstate New York in 1966. These, it was hoped, would right the ship. However, the acrimonious proceedings over whether SNCC should remain an all-black organization overshadowed the programmatic decision to organize local Freedom Organizations. Many left the final cloister feeling that this was no longer their SNCC. I, too, questioned whether SNCC could successfully stake out new ground.

If so, would it be a fit for Bob, Herman, and me? I had another dog in the hunt. I had been summoned for induction into the armed services, as had Bob and Herman. I had sent my declaration of refusal to serve. The three of us accelerated our discussion about fleeing the United States. Family and friends reported they were being harassed by FBI agents. Herman and I were clearly the subjects of heightened surveillance. Leaving the Peg Leg Bates Estate, Herman Carter and I accompanied Bob Moses to Harlem, New York, and soon afterwards crossed the border to Canada.

November 1966, aged nineteen, found me a Vietnam War resister and politically exiled in Canada. We were now underground illegals with newly assumed identities. We had fled the killing fields of the South and the extension of American racism and subjugation into Southeast Asia. Bob Moses would stay in Montreal for two years before leaving for Tanzania. I would not see him again until June 23, 2014. It was the occasion of the Mississippi Freedom Summer 50th

Reunion at Tougaloo College in Jackson, Mississippi. Forty-eight years later.

Herman Carter died in Montreal on January 21, 2018.

### Whose Story Is it Anyway?

> *"There is only one history of any importance, and it is the history of what you once believed in, and the history of what you come to believe in."*
>
> —Kay Boyle, *Words That Must Somehow Be Said: Selected Essays, 1927-1984*.

There are now countless books about SNCC and the myriad prisms through which to view the civil rights movement. Why this one? This one tells the story of my involvement and how that came to be. How my relationships, interactions with significant movement personalities, events and decisions influenced and shaped the course of my life. A journey of unforeseen and unimagined personal dislocations and consequences. The full price of the ticket is still pending. I remain haunted by questions of what happened to so many of our fallen and the few of us still standing, albeit with replaced hips and walking sticks.

I recently revisited the late John Lewis's *Walking with the Wind* and *Across That Bridge* and wrote of our first and subsequent interactions. His dogged championing of voter rights continues to resonate in these draconian times of voter suppression, anti-intellectualism, and antidemocratic impulses. He was not one to seek the headlines or the limelight. However, I know that he would, humbly, accede to his voter registration activities being used to demonstrate the long and bloody road traveled by blacks, and allied whites, to secure the vote. However, his journey was about so much more than the vote and the "good trouble making" tradition that is still required to stand our ground against current efforts to erode past gains and undermine "we the people." It is disheartening to see the emotional outpourings and tributes tailored to suit the cloth of the times—his radicalism and vision manifested in his March on Washington speech and *Across That Bridge* trampled with the revisionist trimmings bestrewing the cutting room floor. He was the fire next time—not the remixed gentle crusader.

A word about the title *Eyes Have Seen*: I have always been fascinated by the notion of seeing and ways of seeing. A cousin of my youth was rumored to be blessed with the sight of caulbearers—supposedly born with an invisible facial veil—empowering her to see the dead. There were times in the darkness of night that she would suddenly halt and point upwards into tree branches.

"Look," she would shout and detail the headless, ghostly presence. I would immediately flee—abandoning her in the dust of my escape. My mother would always insist that I go back and get her. Did I believe that she could see these apparitions? If not, then why flee? Was I blind to the evidence of things unseen?

According to Siri Hustvedt: "Everyone walks on the dead because we walk on the earth."

### Lord, it's a Miracle

> *"Now here we go again, Lord,*
> *We've got to have a Miracle..."*
>
> —Shirley Caesar, *Lord We Need A Miracle* Gospel song (2002)

I remember a young female neighbor suffered a nervous breakdown. She was not speaking, nor eating, losing weight, and not sleeping. Pajama-clad she would escape the house during the night and walk the neighborhood. Her mother grew exhausted keeping vigil. The dad, concerned for both, suggested the daughter be placed in a sanatorium. The mom would not hear of it. She and the grandmother drove her to see a woman in a rural area of New Orleans. The daughter never spoke of the doings. I did not understand what had happened. I could see that she was back to her old self. How did she see things? I don't know. I was always afraid to ask. I dared not risk letting the genie out of the bottle.

What of blind Willis? Inexplicably known as "Man." He was the brother of Mrs. Turner—matriarch of my Greenville host family. "Man" was blind from birth and always hopeful of being sighted. We piled into the car on a sultry summer day and drove to Vicksburg, Mississippi and pulled into the red clay driveway of a backwoods cabin. Mrs. Turner assisted her brother up the steps and into the front door. Only "Man" was allowed inside the anteroom. He emerged, an hour later, unassisted, smiling, pointing, and commenting on the color of the yard fence and the clothing of nearby children at play. He laughed and chatted on the return drive to Greenville. Along the way describing the appearance and colors of roadside flowers. We exchanged looks of incredulity. How was he seeing? Was he really seeing or was he seeing what we willed him to see?

We awoke the next morning to the sounds of "Man" performing his early morning shave. His face and head were bloody with multiple knicks and cuts. He obviously could no longer see.

Teju Cole is one of my favorite authors. An African critic, short story writer, novelist, and a brilliant photographer. His recent offering entitled *Blind Spot* is a twinning of photographs and text. A juxtaposition that raises questions about "What is seeing? What is inside the person looking? What is outside him? How do we parse what we see? Which world? See how? We who?" It is this perspective which informs *Eyes Have Seen*.

I implore the reader to *"shut your eyes and see,"* as instructed by Irish author James Joyce.

# PART I

Map of the State of Mississippi (Julie Benoît)

CHAPTER ONE

# BEGINNINGS

## The Hub City

*"To understand the world, you must first understand a place like Mississippi."*

—William Faulkner (attributed)

*"Who is it that can tell me who I am?"*

—Shakespeare, *King Lear* (1.4.217)

1947 born. 4:40 p.m. 326 Lee Street. Hattiesburg, Mississippi. Forrest County. The county was created from Perry County in 1908 and named in honor of Nathan Forrest—a Confederate General in the American Civil War and an early member, if not founder, of the Ku Klux Klan. Hattiesburg was founded in 1884. It is centrally located about ninety minutes from the state capitol of Jackson, Mississippi and roughly the same distance from New Orleans, Louisiana and Mobile, Alabama. The city gained its nickname, "The Hub City," in 1912: the result of a contest in a local newspaper—so called because it is at the intersection of several famous rail lines. The New Orleans and Northeastern Railroad and the Gulf and Ship Island Railroad. The 1940-50 census cites a population of 29,477.

The caste system of Jim Crow laws stratified the races and was bible to law enforcement and extrajudicial white powers. These laws affected every aspect of daily life from the cradle to the grave. Mandating segregation of schools, parks, libraries, drinking fountains, restaurants, trains, buses, and restrooms. "Whites Only" and "Colored" signs were constant reminders of the enforced racial order.

I was born and raised the second youngest of eight children. I was a mama's boy. I could get privileges unheard of by my older siblings. Likewise, mom knew she could get anything from me. I was a tattletale. Word among the siblings was, "Don't tell Fred or mom will know." We lived in a small house at 326 Lee Street in Newman Quarters. Ours was a medium-income household. I don't ever recall thinking of us as poor. My father worked for the federally subsidized Hercules Powder Company. A company job considered to be among the best available employment opportunities for "Negroes." He was a highly respected and reliable provider.

Dad was of medium height and coffee-hued complexion. He had large, hooded eyes and a head with a receding hairline topped with a bald crown. He always spoke with a few well-chosen words. He was a stutterer which caused him to be reserved and taciturn. He was a meticulous dresser and visited the barbershop every Saturday morning for the obligatory haircut and shoeshine. He walked Mobile Street, hands in pockets, neatly clad in starched khaki pants with a red polka dot handkerchief tucked in his rear pocket with just a hint peeking out and a matching khaki shirt. I proudly walked beside him—peeking tip of a red polka dot handkerchief in the rear of my khaki pants and hands in my pockets. His most cherished pastime was weaving intricately patterned cane bottom chairs. He was an incurable whittler. His bone-handled pocketknife was always against the grain of some fallen tree branch or wind-blown, rain-soaked driftwood.

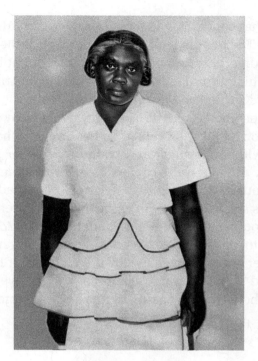

Maggie Anderson, Fred's mother.

Herbert—dad—cultivated crops on the land at the rear of our house. He grew cabbage, lettuce, collard greens, snap and Purvis beans, watermelons, cantaloupes, okra, cucumbers, and peanuts. Everybody called them goobers. One of several African terms for peanuts. I later came to understand that this manifested one instance of linguistic African cultural retention in African American culture. Slave ships had carried crops of peanuts, rice, other grains, okra, and yams to feed their transatlantic slave cargo.

Once, I witnessed another backyard event of African cultural retention. A neighbor expressed anxiety about her baby girl's seemingly late development at walking. My grandmother stood the girl in the backyard, scooped up her footprints in her bandana, and tossed them backwards over her shoulder. The bundle landed on the far side of the chimney and grandmother triumphantly announced that all would be well. This cultural remedy is attributed to the tribes of the Dahomey Kingdom of West Africa, now Benin.

I once nearly severed the heel of my right foot by carelessly stepping on a broken beverage bottle. Grandmother packed my foot with white sugar and bound it with her polka dot bandana. All was well. There was also the time I set out to climb our backyard Chinaberry tree. I first had to climb atop dad's smokehouse by latching onto the gutter. My right hand encountered a wasps' nest and the hand reddened and enlarged to look like a giant ham. Grandmother removed all the stingers, wetted my paw down with some of her garret snuff, and wrapped it in a bandana. All was well. I often wonder about the provenance of this and other practices.

## Maggie

*"They rung my bell to ask me. Could you recommend a maid? I said yes, your momma."*

—Langston Hughes, *Ask Your Momma: 12 Moods for Jazz* (1961)

Mother was a tall, shapely, big-boned woman. She had black but mostly greying hair and brows. Her eyes were like silver lightning, sharp with intelligence and deep set beneath heavy black-greying brows. She seemed to be never without a waist apron which dangled with coins secreted in a knotted fold. She always chewed spearmint gum. The scent of which, all these years later, never fails to bring me to tears. She was not one to speak endearments. However, her touch was soft and feathery and there were gestures that conveyed gentleness and affection. Especially when she moistened your face with Royal

Crown jelly and stood back, hands on hips, inspecting, after tucking and straightening your necktie for Sunday school. I could see the smile of admiration—just prideful enough not to be sinful. Her smiling presence filled the door frame as she ushered you off to school. The lingering elbow nearness as she surreptitiously ladled an extra serving of my favorite dish. How she wordlessly rolled down the covers, smoothed the sheets, crimped the pillows, lifted you—swaddle-tucked the covers and stood in the doorway gazing until quietly closing my bedroom door.

Mom was a domestic worker, keeping house for a local white woman. She did the cleaning, laundry, and cooking of meals. I remember once joking that all the black maids had the power to wipe out the white population by food poisoning. She laughed and cautioned me to never, ever, let anybody hear me say such a thing. Ironically, she had full access to the house of employment but could not enter through the front door. I sometimes accompanied her to work as it was my summer job to mow the spacious front and rear lawns. I would often see mom wave through the kitchen window. I was not allowed in the house. Mom would prepare and serve my lunch on the back-porch steps. Supper was always late in Newman Quarters because many of the domestics had to first serve supper to their white households. It helped that dad could hold his own in the kitchen. This is, no doubt, the genesis of my love for cooking. My mother also assisted in the management of a local shop owned by my grandfather.

She was the family disciplinarian. There were never more welcoming words than "I am too tired. I will let your father deal with you." But that didn't happen the day I accompanied my boyhood friend J.C. to the forbidden swimming hole. Neither of us were adequate swimmers. J.C. ventured too far out. I glimpsed his head low in the water. His mouth open at water level. Eyes glassy and empty, unable to focus. I frantically dog-paddled out. But I was too late. The surface of the lake was undisturbed. Eerily calm. He was gone. I was gasping for air, a fluttering, racing feeling.

I flailed myself onto land, rushed home, and joined friends on the softball field. Others would come later announcing news of the drowning. I acknowledged nothing. I had failed to notice there were fishermen on the far shore. They were the source of the breaking news. The fishermen had called the fire department and the body was recovered. I went home consumed by fear and dread. My mother soon returned from work and was in conversation with neighbors at our front gate. I could hear the ladies say proper authorities had placed me at the scene of the tragedy. I could also see mom's body stiffen and her gaze shifting toward the house. Never was there such a beating. My wailing could be heard across the neighborhood. My grandmother, alarmed, rushed to the house, and commanded my mother to cease. I did not want to attend the funeral. But mother insisted. I am glad she did. I owed that much to J.C. Still, all these years later, I struggle to awake from night terrors. The glassy, unseeing eyes of J.C.

There was another significant beating. I especially enjoyed the companionship of Uncle Johnny. He was what we called jet black, which earned him the nickname "Midnight." It is him that I am rumored to most resemble.

Uncle Johnny was an avid hunter. He taught me how to care for and shoot the Winchester rifle. We tracked and shot rabbits, partridge, quail, wild turkeys, and deer. He was also known to be a gambler and bootlegger of bourbon whiskey. Mississippi was a dry state. I would frequently ride along in the bootlegging truck to New Orleans. He was always armed. Not to confront sheriffs or deputies but to protect us from pilfering white vigilantes. He would always visit the gambling houses. Upstairs he would go. I remained seated in the parlor and would eventually succumb to sleep. Early morning footsteps and boisterous voices ended my sleep. We breakfasted on fluffy biscuits with gravy, grits and shrimp, and fried oysters. The truck would rumble across the Lake Pontchartrain Causeway towards Hattiesburg.

Things eventually went awry. My uncle decided to use my two cousins and me as mules to sell booze at the local football games. We were outfitted with coats equipped with multiple false pockets. He provided money to purchase game tickets. However, Cousin Jason decided to maximize our profits by scaling the stadium fence. An enriching idea except that Cousin Clarence got entangled. One of his bottles tumbled below and broke on the asphalt pathway. We were suddenly ablaze in the glare of security agents' flashlights. They quick-stepped us to the security office. A phone call was placed. I was informed that my mom was coming to collect us. It was a hide-blistering comeuppance. It would be some time before she would speak to my uncle, her brother, again.

Also notable, was the grocery store incident. A school friend pocketed three barely concealed oranges. We were seized.

"Fred, why are you stealing oranges?" asked mom.

"I didn't, mom. I don't even like oranges," I pleaded.

"Well,"—twirling the belt—"you will hate them now," she pronounced.

"But mom, I didn't do anything wrong," I averred.

"Except acting like a fool. Everybody in Newman Quarters but you knows that the other boy is a thief," she parried.

Ours was a close-knit community of strong men and even stronger women. Every mother was your mother. All were empowered to administer an ass whipping and send you homeward where the next ass whipping awaited. We were surrounded by mom's and dad's sisters and brothers. All living alongside or in the rear of our house. My grandparents resided two houses down at 116 Lee Street.

Aunt Lula Johnson-Conner. Family stalwart.
(Photo courtesy of Elizabeth Edwards)

Their home was referred to as "the big house." It was the nerve center for family gatherings and emergencies. Grandfather was the presiding patriarch. It was always fun to be there unless summoned to a personal audience with him and his admonition of "Dog gon' your picture." Meaning damn the likes of you.

My aunt Lula was the proprietor of a hair salon located at the rear of the property. She was the matriarch of our clan. She was stout and fierce. Her mouth and smile glistened with a studded gold tooth crown. She possessed a scathing sense of humor and a pistol to back it up. Especially when it honed-in on something that irritated her, like her preternatural disdain of "white folk." Never more so than when her gaze gyroscoped and her electric eel of a tongue lassoed, "Ironing board, flat-butted, stringy-haired white women." The ladies would abandon their chairs and howl with hyena-like guffaws and knee-bowed genuflecting.

"They ain't worth the heartache or the lynching. You heah me boy," she warned.

Aunt Lula was renowned for the ability to ensure that you were, if need be, remembered stylistically in death as you had been in life. I earned some small change sweeping her floor of sheared locks. The shop was bulging with girls and women of all ages, shapes, and styles. The conversations and memories flowed amidst the smoking blue curlers, the sizzling hot combs, singed hair and assorted kink-busting products from the line and lineage of the black millionaire heiress Madame C.J. Walker. The salon was a beehive of salacious disclosures. An unanticipated youthful glimpse into the adult goings-on in the quarters. Aunt Lula would frequently hush and remind that "my young ears should be spared the inner workings of female preoccupations."

The Gaston family house was a hop and skip from us. Their son Clifford was my schoolmate and best friend. Clifford had mustard-tone skin. He was muscled, mercurial, and protective of me and boyhood friends. He was, seemingly, always bloody nosed, shrouded in a cloud of dust, elbowing, butting heads, kicking, ear biting, flailing away, and warding off real and imaginary foes. He was always packing a boy scout knife and brass knuckles.

Walter was a kid burdened with congenital hydrocephalus. His enlarged head was the size of a prize-winning watermelon. He was called 'water head' and mercilessly teased by some crosstown kids and stopped going to school. Clifford spoke with his mom and volunteered to be his school escort, and the bullying quickly stopped.

I was convinced that Clifford would perish in an automobile accident. His dad's pick-up truck was pockmarked like the lunar surface of the moon. Neighborhood windows cracked from wheel-churned gravel; the truck careening and tilting dangerously like a ship against a stiff wind. He rode his bicycle in the same "hi-yo-silver-and-away-we-go" fashion. He was perpetually involved in head-tossed-over-handlebars crashes and proudly sported his scar trophies.

I later learned that he had to flee Hattiesburg to Boston, Massachusetts. He had refused to be seated at the back of the bus and the enraged driver confronted him and attempted to shove him off the bus. Clifford brass knuckled the driver's head. He was arrested and fled town. I would learn much later that he had escaped an accidental death.

He died in Vietnam. Perhaps rushing recklessly into an enemy fire storm protecting a brother from the neighborhood. "One Never Knows, Do One?" asked the legendary Thomas "Fats" Waller.

Ella, his mom, and I had a unique relationship. We shared a common bond of civil rights experiences. Her story and our relationship are recounted in the epilogue of Pam Johnson's book, *Justice For Ella: A Story That Needed To Be Told* (2014) which chronicles the unlikely partnership and resistance of two Hattiesburg women, white and black, who teamed up in the 1950s and embraced clandestine activities to thwart the arrest of Ella. Ella's history of fighting racism was longstanding and would continue to find expression in her acting as the secret conduit for my exiled messages to my family.

### A Childhood Harvest

> *"For everything there is a season."*
>
> —Ecclesiastes 3:1 KJV

Henry, my grandfather, was a mid-scale farmer. He grew crops for subsistence and the market. I always looked forward to joining him in the fields. Planting corn, potatoes, tomatoes, assorted beans, squash, cucumbers, variegated greens, sugarcane, and watermelons. I especially liked the harvest time. We took breaks to eat sweet potatoes baked in the ashes of a wood fire. Butter dripping hoecake—a biscuit-like batter fried on the heated hoe blade and smoldering-ash-roasted corn. I would swoon in anticipation of the sweet running juices of watermelon and sugarcane. I recall sitting alongside him atop the hitched mule wagon as he drove the dusty backroads, delivering provisions to our less fortunate neighbors. Grandfather also raised livestock. The cows and hogs were slaughtered for family consumption.

Grandmother was the homemaker. She was always seized with canning preserves and making jams. Her woodburning stove was perpetually stoked, endlessly gurgling pots of food. I would often dash home in pursuit of the wafting aroma that signaled the making of molasses. The big wood-fired boiling pot in the center of the backyard and Dinah, the mule, hitched to a tourniquet squeezing the green and yellowed cane stalks. The silky sweet juice gliding down the trough into the roiling cauldron. Sometimes I was allowed to ride or lead the stubborn mule and coerce its circular plodding—twisting the cane to pulp and the flow of juice. The cavernous pot was also used to make lye soap and pork crackling.

Winter hog-killing time was always the best of boyhood fun. Neighbors would assemble to watch my grandfather nudge the wary pig into the narrow confines of the shute. He would fell the pig by striking the head with the blunt back end of an axe. Grandmother would stoke the wood-fired black pot to a high boil. The pig would be fully immersed in the scalding water and the hairs and bristles removed by vigorously scraping the hide with jagged clay bricks. Grandfather used his bone-handled knife to carve slits to expose the elastic tendons in the rear legs. The white, naked carcass would be hung in dangling suspension from wooden pegs attached to the big barn and smokehouse. The steel blue glinting blade slashed the throat, and a gashed laceration of gurgling blood drained into the basin. Grandmother would transform the bright translucent stream into blood sausages. The pig would be hosed with high-velocity water, belly slit open from head to tail, and thoroughly washed with vinegar and water. Neighborhood men would assist in butchering sections of ham, hocks, tenderloins, baby back and long ribs, pork belly, neck bones, fatback, shoulder, and companion roasts. The head was severed for hog head cheese, tail and feet for soups, hooves for home remedy tea, and intestines for chitlins. The hams would be herbed, dressed, hung, smoked, and cured. The other sections would be encased in salt and stored in the barn for the winter and later use.

Nothing was wasted. The lord is good.

### Keeper of Tales, Mistress of Poultices

*"The axe forgets; the tree remembers."*

—African Proverb

Grandmother also managed a large cluster of noisy and aggressive chickens. The hatchery provided poultry and eggs.

My grandparents were, in appearance, an unlikely couple. She was a snuff dipper, short in stature, and a dabbler in enchantments. I never saw her hair—it was always cloaked beneath a polka-dotted bandana. She was a perpetual motion machine, always beating rugs, taking in wash, or turning soil and pruning flowers. Grandfather, on the other hand, was strikingly tall, splendorous in dress and had chiseled features accentuated by horn-rimmed spectacles. He was always topped with a grey felt fedora.

He was earthy, unhurried in his movements, and would warn me not to listen to the profane foolishness of my grandmother. However, there was an irresistible tow to the liquid, green-tinted bottles of her potions and the fiendish invocations which accompanied her gathering of roots and bark. The sacred and ritualistic tone in which she spoke and acknowledged oblation to the tree. Her strong hands snapped a piece of bark in half.

"Take a bite. What does it taste like?" she wanted to know.

"I don't taste nothing," I ventured.

She grew frustrated. "Well, as much as you like to climb trees and drink root beer, you sure don't know nothing about trees," she opined. She continued sterilizing jars and used a tiny syringe to mix liquids of many hues.

A neighbor lady entered the yard. There was a whispered consultation.

"Come here. Take this key, go in the cellar, and bring me one of those tiny green bottles from the middle shelf. Don't touch nothing else and come right back up outta there and make sure that you lock the door behind you," she commanded.

I was stunned. No one other than her, as far as I knew, had been allowed to cross the threshold. Her swollen legs were bothering her, perhaps. It was a large pantry. I had to bushwhack my way through densely matted cobwebs. A single ceiling light bulb shone dimly in the darkness. There were shelves upon shelves of bottles. There were large vats filled with fermenting blackberries, peaches, muscadine grapes, and dandelion weeds. There was a long, smaller shelf on the opposite wall. I pulled the cork of a large crock jar. It was peach brandy. There was a cast iron pot atop a burner plate. Used, no doubt, to boil down and distill the healing powers. There was a large cedar wood trunk and credenza against the wall. But I resisted the urge to rummage. I needed to get above ground.

"What took you so long?" she barked. She held the bottle up to the sunlight, squinted and wiped away the dust, mumbled some form of incantation and secreted the bottle into the folds of her apron. None of the bottles were labeled because grandmother could not write or read. I knew this because she would often ask me to read her letters, on those occasions when she could not delay gratification until my aunt Jessie, Lula, Irma, or my mother got home.

"I can teach you to read, grandma," I offered.

"Who said I can't read? Just because I like to hear you read. Don't mean I can't read," she snapped. "Go on and read me the letter," she commanded. It was a letter from Michigan. One of her sons—my uncle Samuel. Some of the content was not for my young eyes.

"You don't know nothing about that. Do you?" she would ask me.

"About what, grandma?" I would ask in reply.

"I didn't think you did." She would wink. "Take this nickel and buy yourself some of that lockjaw candy."

Francis, as grandmother was called, cultivated the most wondrous flowers. She was the florist of Newman Quarters. Generously gifting blossoms on births, weddings, birthdays, illnesses, and deaths. She was also a master quiltmaker. Women elders gathered around her considerable quilting frame, selected their fragments of fabric, earned seating, and went to work. I have searched in vain for one of my grandmother's quilts. Aching for the embracing succor of her stitched memories. Their warmth and adorning beauty. They were her medium of personal expression—transmitting culture. A means of connecting generations and creating community.

The assembled women were all of failing sight. It was my boyhood task to maintain an ample supply of threaded needles which afforded me the privilege of listening as they spun tales of local heroes, heroines, and the tragedies that had befallen so many of our race. John Hartfield lynched in Ellisville, Mississippi, twenty miles north of Hattiesburg (June 1926). Emmett Till, fourteen-year-old black teenager, beaten to death by a group of white vigilantes (August 1955) in Money, Mississippi. Accused and vanquished. Twenty-three years old, Mack Charles Parker (April 24, 1959), also accused of raping a white woman. He was arrested and abducted, under the cover of darkness, from the county jail in Poplarville, Mississippi, beaten, shot twice in the chest, and dumped into the Pearl River—forty minutes north of Hattiesburg. Corporal Roan Duckworth, a black GI military policeman shot and killed by white policemen in Taylorsville, Mississippi (April 1962), mistaken as a freedom rider. He was on the way to the hospital for the birth of his sixth child— one hour and fifteen minutes northwest of Hattiesburg. Clyde Kennard of Hattiesburg—army veteran—pioneered the desegregation of higher education in Mississippi. He applied multiple times to attend the campus of Mississippi Southern College (now University of Southern Mississippi). Clyde was arrested and imprisoned in 1960 on the fabricated charge of stealing chicken feed. He was granted early release in 1963 due to advanced stages of leukemia and died soon afterwards. These were just a few of the known.

My grandmother would sum up the litany, saying, "Yes, Lord. Many thousands gone." A mournful refrain of a timeless Negro Spiritual. This dirge of atrocities overhung Newman Quarters—a hovering, menacing cloud of fear.

## Storm Clouds Gather

*"Blues Walking like a Man."*
—Robert Johnson, *Preaching Blues* (1939)

My aunt Irma was crying and beckoning mom to join her on the front porch. Aunts and uncles had been urgently summoned to the big house. I could see them hurriedly passing our living room window—some at a fast gait and others running. Mom and dad joined the cavalcade.

They returned hours later and reported that our teenage cousin Sammy Johnson, Jr. was dead. I had never seen mom or dad cry. Cousin Sammy was returning home from a Boy Scouts expedition to Waveland, Mississippi. He stopped to say hello to our grandparents. Home for Sammy was across town in another section of the black community. He—we—always shortened the distance by walking the alleyway behind the Inn, a locally owned redneck establishment. Sammy never made it home.

The police report said that he had been "eyeing" a white woman through the window of the inn. The police approached. He fled and was shot multiple times in the back, suffering a broken neck by colliding with a fence post. None of us believed this account. Sammy's father—residing in Michigan arranged for the body to be transported by train. Lawyers were retained and an independent autopsy was performed, which contradicted the police report. Sammy had been riddled with bullets to his front and rear and had sustained multiple broken bones in his arms and legs, resulting from a blunt force instrument. His dad contracted the services of the Mississippi chapter of the National Association for the Advancement of Colored People (NAACP).

I do not to this day know the outcome of this incident, though speculation abounds. I frequently asked my older sister Mary what happened. She does not exactly know but believes the case stalled because a relative provided "suspect information" to the NAACP lawyers. However, the one clear outcome is that this horror—this trauma—forever marked me.

My mother could sense my recoil and was concerned that I might act out in a manner that would put me and others at risk. I overheard her asking my father whether I should be sent to live with relatives in the North. Away from the indignities of whites-only and colored-only signs for public toilets and water fountains. Away from the demeaning reductions of takeout services at the side window of restaurants. Away from the no trying-on of clothing because no white person would purchase anything that had touched a black body. Away from balcony-only seating in the theatre—derisively referred to as "nigger heaven." Away from the feet shuffling and hats-off honorific of surrendering the sidewalk to allow unimpeded access to whites. Away from boarding the back of the bus—the "colored section"—and the compounding contumely of being squeezed further to the back to accommodate surplus white passengers; black children and elders surrendering their seats and standing. Away from the obsequious eyes-down kabuki dance to approaching white women, to protect the black body against allegations of ogling them.

Still, it was home, and I did not want to leave my friends, school, and relatives. I especially did not wish to be separated from mom. She reluctantly respected my wishes after extracting a promise that I would not be challenging the local whites. Mothers were acutely aware that, despite their primordial instincts to protect their young, there was a more lethal white predatory presence that could snatch us away. Especially their sons. Increasing numbers of parents were sending their sons to the North to live with relatives. Schoolmates were in class one day and gone the next.

## If Mobile Street Could Talk

We remained, despite the omnipresent white glare, a proud and resilient community. The central antidote against racism's daily encroachments was the long-established historic Mobile-Bouie Street black business district. It was one of Mississippi's most influential nexuses of black entrepreneurship, professional life, and commerce, and would soon become a fulcrum of civil rights activism radiating across the state and the nation. This bustling Mobile-Bouie Street thoroughfare had doctors, dentists, tailors, grocery stores, a bank, movie theatre, cafes, pool hall, barbershops, dry cleaners, hardware store, beauty salons, boarding houses, clothing emporium, a hotel, and two funeral homes—the most renowned being Clarke Funeral Home. Immortalized by our irreverent childhood chant: "God's gonna bless you, but Clarke gonna dress you." And Smith's Drug Store, home to a soda fountain and the best cones of swirling soft dairy ice cream.

It was by way of Mobile Street, family, churches, schools, and other black institutions that we received alternative messaging shielding us against efforts to inculcate a conception of ourselves as inferior to whites. We were always reminded by parents and elders that it did not matter if you had to be a ditch digger but be the best ditch digger in the world. Jarvis Givens described the tradition of black education as "fugitive pedagogy" and seditious from its inception. (Jarvis Givens, *Fugitive Pedagogy: Carter G. Woodson and the Art of Black Teaching*.) Cleanliness and good manners were obligatory. The guiding ethos of Newman Quarters found expression in the pillars of family, church, and school.

Mt. Bethel Baptist Church was located on the hilltop at the end of our red clay street. Directly opposite the snow cone shop. The ungodly recipient of my Sunday offerings. Services

Mt. Bethel Baptist Church, Newman Quarters,
Hattiesburg, Mississippi. Scene of joy and heartbreak.
(Photo courtesy of Elizabeth Edwards)

were twice daily. Early morning Sunday school for the young and afternoon service for all. Sunday school provided bible instruction—each supplicant was required to recite a bible verse. I inexorably quoted "Jesus wept." The shortest verse in the bible. Grandmother would remind me that Jesus could not have accomplished all his miracles had he spent so much time crying.

Sundays were an occasion for best dress, delicious foods, and soul-stirring gospel singing. Above all else was the observance of best behavior. God did not have it within all his omnipotence to save or forgive misbehavior in church. Your ass belonged to mom.

## ABCs of Race

*"A Mind Is a Terrible Thing to Waste."*

—United Negro College Fund (1972)

Our schooling was rigorous despite the inequalities in funding and teachers' pay. We studied and learned from tattered, hand-me-down textbooks and science lab equipment from the white schools. The books were sometimes missing pages and inscribed with racial epithets. We had talented teachers that demanded attentiveness and excellence. Many of our teachers had gained their degrees at Cornell University, University of Chicago, Northwestern University, Indiana University, Howard, Lincoln, Columbia University, and other institutions.

My brother and math tutor, Herbert Anderson, Jr., graduated from Indiana University. He would eventually be appointed Professor of Mathematics and Dean of Students at the Alcorn State University, a Historically Black College or University (HBCU).

Herbert was taller than tall and straighter than an arrow. He combed and precision-parted his steel wool hair to the sides. He had served duty in the U.S. Navy and would snap to attention and salute the national anthem as it sounded on the television screen. He was a cigar smoker who spoke gruffly. I relished the run to purchase cigars and his reward of a shiny Indian-headed dime. He dated my grade-school teacher and frequently came by the school to take her to lunch. He arrived once as I was being disciplined by standing in the corner facing the wall. Ostrich-like on one leg.

Our teachers were our neighbors. We shopped together, went to church, rubbed shoulders at picnics, funerals, sporting events, and other community activities. They cared about us. Inspired and pushed us and expected nothing less than the best. I was a good, sometimes mischievous, student. Teachers were always reminding me that my brothers and sisters had been through the same schools, sat in the same classroom with the same teachers—always forewarning that I could not let the family tradition down.

I was a voracious and insatiable reader. Blacks did not have access to the local library; northern relatives nurtured my reading by mail ordered books. I grew familiar with black and white authors across the United States. Mississippi author Richard Wright's *Black*—a childhood tale of growing up black in Mississippi was a sonorous and lifesaving read.

Mrs. Chambers taught social studies. She would lace her lessons with clandestine civics and constitutional rights and voting long before local blacks were allowed to vote in numbers. We called her "the hawk" because she never failed to observe back-turned school antics. Mrs. Weathersby was a former Presbyterian missionary that had served in Liberia and other African countries. She taught current affairs and dispelled many of the prevailing myths and distortions about Africa.

Mrs. Hopson and Mrs. Sandifer taught English. I came to love the appreciation of words and their power to make the listener see colors, smells, and be touched by the vibrations of words.

Mrs. Nicholson was responsible for shepherding the annual student school speech. She would often present me at school assemblies to recite my poetry and essays. Most of which declaimed on black pride and the need for social change in Hattiesburg—causing schoolmates to tag me with the nickname "black flag." Mrs. Nicholson was relentlessly promoting and guiding my choices for higher education.

## As Quick as You Can Say Jackie Robinson

> *"They used to say, 'If we find a good Black player, we'll sign him.' They was lying."*
>
> —Cool Papa Bell, preeminent Negro League Baseball player

My passion was baseball. I yearned to play for the Hattiesburg Black Sox. The club was located just outside of Hattiesburg in Palmers Crossing. The all-black outfit was inaugurated in 1941—a cog in the wheel of the Independent Negro League—and would not become an integrated team until the mid-1980s.

The Sox's games were a major community event. The bleachers would always be packed. Including some adventuresome whites. I never missed their practices or games. My eyes were always fixated on the catcher. He was only known by his initials of R.C. He would, during the warm-up, catch throws from the outfield behind his back or through the legs and no would-be Jackie Robinson dared attempt stealing third base on his watch. He could unleash his cannon throw from the famed rocking-chair, feet swiveling position.

I was mostly a catcher in little league play but remained undecided on which position to pursue in advanced league play until R.C. became my mentor. He devoted countless hours to tutoring and honing my back-stopper skills. I accompanied the team to many games, always observing and asking annoying questions.

Gameday in Tylertown, Mississippi: bottom of the eighth. Black Sox up by six runs, and R.C. says, "You're in." I would now be the Sox's in-training catcher, and my boyhood chum Clifford would become the centerfielder.

But there would be game-changing events. Mother suffered a stroke resulting in diminished mobility in her left arm and leg, and seriously impaired speech. It was hard for me to witness her sadness and frustration. She would eventually recover due primarily to my brother Robert. He put her through the paces of all his athletic training routines. I thought him relentless and cruel; I would tell him so and leave the house. It was too unbearable watching her tears of frustration. But she regained some mobility and improved speech.

Robert, as always, had done what was necessary. Robert was also tall. He had the chiseled body of an athlete, which is what he was. He was debonair, always dressed in razor-edged creased trousers, mooned by a swash-buckle belt that screamed, "Look at my muscle-rippled abdomen." His one imperfection was two wide-gapped front teeth. However, this was not enough to turn away his legion of female admirers. We used to mercilessly tease him during the Christmas holidays, sing-songing, "All I want for Christmas is my two front teeth," until mom flashed the look meaning *enough*.

He was a star wide receiver on the famed high school football squad coached by Ed Steele and Roy Hill. Awarded a scholarship, he would soon leave home to play football for Jackson State College.

Ruby, my older sister, left home to study at Mississippi Valley State College. She was also of tall stature. She was smart but of few words. There was always an "over-the-rainbow" glint in her eyes.

Sister Mary was made of sterner stuff. She was flint-rock hardened with piercing eyes and flaring nostrils. She became pregnant in high school and gave birth to a baby boy named Gregory. The father lived across the street from us. He turned out to be an abuser. Mary returned home late one night with eyes horribly blackened and swollen purple-black lips. Mary didn't say a mumbling word. Mom and dad were apoplectic. The police were not summoned. White police in Hattiesburg didn't give a pinch of salt about crime within our community.

## Tambourines to Glory

Saturday mornings were a ritualistic day in Newman Quarters. The sun was high and warm. The front porches were bathed in shadows. A cool breeze caressed the lilacs and honeysuckles. Mothers sat, daughters and nieces hunched between their legs, oiling faces, legs, and arms, combing, brushing hair, and weaving ancestral patterns of corn rows. Young boys tossed backyard horseshoes. Some girls, released from the hair tugging, twirled, and skipped rope. The ring of hammers and the buzz of handsaws hummed at home repairs. Other T-shirt-clad men played checkers atop the hood of a pick-up truck. The ice truck rolled into the neighbor's front yard. The iceman's large iron tongs grasped a block of ice as he grimaced up the steps. Mary chatted in the across-the-street yard with her boyfriend. The two were talking and laughing as if there were better days ahead.

The idyllic calm and illusion of better days to come was suddenly shattered by screams of horror. All eyes pivoted to the other side of the street. The boyfriend lay crumpled on the ground. There was an ever-expanding gurgling pool of blood. Mary had triggered the release button of her switchblade knife, cut him down to size and gutted him like a bottom-feeding catfish.

Later, under the cover of darkness, grandma and mom led Mary down the back laneway to Uncle Johnny's house. He was already seated in his 1957 eggshell-blue Ford Thunderbird. Grandmother extracted from her bosom a wad of cash which smelled of fresh cut flowers and aged green bottles. She handed the money to Uncle Johnny. He revved the motor. Mary climbed in the back seat, and they sped off for Akron, Ohio, leaving me and her son, Gregory, to share a room and a pee-soaked bed. It was a sad day for the family when she returned to claim him. We had become soulmates. As for

Mary, even to this day, as she lay dying, her greeting of "hey boy," could reduce me to tears. I invariably replied, "hey girl." Nothing else needed to be said.

The ladies at the quilting bee said that they were glad, for him and his family, that he had survived. Grandma emphatically spat juices from her garret snuff into her recycled Crisco lard spittoon and wiped the lip spittle away with the tip of her apron. "I would have loved to cut some flowers for his death box," she said.

Reverend E.W. Rhone figured the incident was a teachable moment—a God-sent parable for his Sunday service. "Sin is sin. Two wrongs don't make a right," he croaked. His voice crescendo-singing and concluding on the downbeat. "This is the work of the devil. It is clear as the heavenly light. Bartimaeus, blind as a bat, can see the fingerprints of diabolical Satan writ large in blood. And I can tell you that God don't like ugly," he trumpeted in apparent reference to Mary.

Mom rose from her pew. "And it would appear that he doesn't care much for pretty either," she retorted and walked out the church door. The large-bosomed, talcum-powdered, over perfumed church matrons were aghast. Their cardboard funeral-home-issued handheld fans paused in midair. I chased after mom.

"You go on back to church. I need you to tell me what all those cooped up cackling hens had to say about me," she ordered.

I went back to church, but it was impossible to listen to the piety and self-righteousness. He was no longer the Reverend Rhone that had lifted me from my pew. Pied-piping me to reluctantly join my peers in a cavalcade of surrendered souls. Not the Reverend Rhone that swathed my trembling body in the white sheet. Bound my head with white handkerchief. Placed his anointing hand over my nose and mouth and dunked me into the waters of the shoulder-high baptismal pool. Not the Reverend Rhone that prayed so long for the redemption of my sinner soul that I feared that he had forgotten me—that I would, like J.C., drown for Jesus—until I broke the surface spouting jets of water like a humpback whale. This Reverend Rhone was all fire and brimstone. Totally lacking in charity. No longer the Reverend Rhone which we children watched with diminishing hopes as he swooped carrion-like and gulped the best pieces of mom's Sunday fried chicken.

Mom never lost her faith. But it was this sermon on this Sunday that Reverend Rhone metaphorically choked on the chicken and drowned my faith.

The house now consisted of my sisters, Johnnie Mae, Thelma, baby sister Sheliah, and myself. Ruby, Herbert, and Robert were away at school and Mary was starting anew in Ohio. Defiant "last word" Thelma was wiry and determined. Mom didn't like her girls participating in sports. Thelma was a high school basketball athlete and, despite whatever punishment, always showed up at game time. Mom eventually acquiesced. Thelma and I were always in a battle of wills. You could hold her head underwater and she would emerge gurgling bubbles and infuriatingly gasping the final word. This is in no way meant to be critical but an acknowledgement of her drive not to be silenced. To be heard.

And there is younger sister Sheliah. The source of much guilt because I abandoned her to join the civil rights movement. Our bonding remains fragile and a work in progress.

Mom would soon succumb to kidney failure, and all would return for her funeral. Eight children; forty-nine years old and gone. I accompanied Aunt Lula and grandmother to Clarke Funeral Home. I sat on a stool, back turned, as the undertakers put her into her favorite dress. I was then allowed to turn around. Aunt Lula styled her hair, applied makeup, arranged earrings, a pearl necklace, wedding band, and

Niece, Natasha Biddings, Sisters Thelma, Mary, Fred, Sisters Sheliah, Ruby, in Akron, Ohio. (Photo courtesy of B.J.)

watch. The attendants placed her in the coffin of dad's choice.

She was, as ever, alive in her beauty. Real. Breathful until the lid was lowered.

"She won't be able to breathe," I said with horror.

My grandmother shot me a look. "This is hard for everybody. No need to make it harder," she warned.

"I won't," I squeaked.

But I did. Days later, as viewers filed past, I impeded the flow as I stood gazing into her coffin. Transfixed. Immovable. Aunt Lula maneuvered behind me.

"Fred. You need to return to the pew," she whispered. She placed a gentle hand on my shoulder and jolted my butt cheek with the sharp prick of her hat pin. My guide in sorrow. Otherwise, I might still be rooted in place. Standing sentinel.

I am, all these years later and in so many ways, still frozen in that moment. It was the saddest day of my young life.

Mom entombed in dirt. Ruby, Robert, Herbert, Jr., and Mary returning to their distant domiciles and other pursuits. Dad would eventually remarry, and Sheliah would struggle with the challenges of a blended family. She eventually married and migrated—joining the other sisters in Akron, Ohio. She is now a single mother of two handsome, well-mannered, college graduated twin boys. But the scars run deep. I was gone during her formative years, and we continue to work diligently, non-judgmentally, to make up for lost time—to bridge the divide of our bifurcated beginnings. It is painful and I recognize that it is my reckoning—my cross to bear. She is now approaching seventy years of age. Taller than me and crowned with a long mane of gray braided strands of hair and her voice sounding most like mom's.

Robert leaving for Jackson State College presented me, through his intercession, a written offer of a scholarship upon graduation to study and play baseball at Tennessee State College. I would soon be an eleventh grader—a beneficiary of advancement from seventh to eighth and tenth to eleventh grade. However, I remained unsettled and undecided about my academic future. Dad did his best with support from surrounding family and neighbors to hold the family together. But mom had been our primary fixative and I could no longer bear to walk the hallways or stomach reminders of her absence. I took to staying with grandparents and aunts. Dad would visit and encourage me to return home, which I eventually did.

In retrospect, I was petulant, insufferable, and lacking sensitivity to dad's loss and grief. My only plausible mitigating circumstance was that I was sagging under the weight of losing the lodestar of my youth. Teachers and elders were encouraging me to stay focused and graduate high school, but my eyes were elsewhere.

Jim Crow Laws made integrated facilities illegal.
These included libraries, beaches, pools, and amusement
parks where blacks were banned.
(Photo courtesy of Herschel Kaminsky)

## I Got Wings

The public airways were full of televised images of a new consciousness and rising black protests. Spring of 1960, the sit-in movement was front-page and television news; telecasting stark images of African American students seated at white segregated lunch counters in Greensboro, North Carolina—denied service and refusing to leave until served. Their efforts met with physical brutality and arrests. I sat stunned and sickened by the images of the white mobs beating, burning buses, and jailing freedom riders.

Hattiesburg would soon be impacted by the aftershocks of this new phase of protest in the civil rights movement. Hollis Watkins, Curtis Hayes, and MacArthur Cotton arrived in Hattiesburg in 1962. Their arrival, and that of Bob Moses and others, signaled the beginning of the modern-day civil rights struggle in Hattiesburg. I felt a tug of kinship. Hattiesburg blacks had always historically banded together to improve their lives. However, this community organizing tradition was unlike the previous onslaughts against Jim Crow. The SNCC insurgents arrived armed with essential contacts and the benefits of the previous resistant efforts of local leadership, but it would require months of painstaking efforts to gain trust in the broader community. Many doors would be slammed in their faces and many churches would deny their entreaties for meeting places.

CHAPTER TWO

# A BAND OF BROTHERS AND SISTERS

## Circle of Trust

> *"How could such a beginning ringed in water, come to such an end fixed in fire?"*
>
> —Thomas King, *77 Fragments of a Familiar Ruin* (2019)

Word spread quickly that there were "freedom riders," "outsiders," or "troublemakers" in the community. Parents and elders cajoled from front porches and church deacons warned us to stay clear.

I first came to know of the voter mobilization meeting through my sister Johnnie Mae. We were sitting on our front porch watching girls at play. Keeping time to the tick-tat patter beneath their bare-footed toes as they double-Dutch skipped between two twirling ropes. Johnnie Mae asked if I wanted to go. I did but was surprised as this was the first sign of my sister's interest. Johnnie Mae was named for our uncle Johnny, except for the letter Y, and was a girl of no surprises; an under-the-radar goody two-shoes, which suited her just fine. She was of stout build, dark complexion, and could run on quicksand. She had exceptionally bright teeth, a broad smile, and a guttural rumbling and infectious laugh.

We set out early evening and took the long route to avoid the Inn—the site of the police killing of Cousin Sammy. The Morning Star Baptist church steps were full of people with SNCC workers jubilantly leading the crowd in the chorus of a freedom song "Ain't Gonna Let Nobody Turn Me Around." White men in trucks—gun racks visible—circled the church. Police cars and fire trucks wheeled by with blaring sirens. Inside, the church was near full. It was a time of "testifying" of a different kind. Not about how I found Jesus, but about previous voter registration attempts, racial harassment, and the sure knowledge of the impending personal and collective retribution that awaited the end of the meeting. Firemen rushed in falsely claiming that there was a fire. But all stood firm, defiantly singing, "Just like a tree, planted by the water, we shall not be moved."

We started the long walk home, trailed by a police car with dimmed headlights slowly tracking us. We walked in silence. Holding hands until the cruiser veered off. We knew without speaking that this was an experience that we could only talk of amongst ourselves. We would later hear of others that had lost jobs and business licenses because of the gathering.

I was impressed with the courage and commitment of the SNCC workers. Their ability to connect the dots required to rise above fear and paralysis and calm the nervous gathering—to succinctly showcase the small, doable acts of courage. As a result, I joined the campaign to recruit voters and would undergo hours of training. We canvassed neighborhoods, knocking on doors, educating, and convincing people to register and vote in the mock elections. We tirelessly revisited hesitant neighbors. In the first week of November 1963, 83,000 black Mississippians cast their ballots in churches, beauty parlors, barbershops, pool halls, and lodges. A hundred northern white ministerial representatives from the National

Council of Churches arrived in Mississippi to observe and certify the legitimacy of the vote.

The ministers also attended local white churches encouraging moderate white voices to support decency and restraint. Many of us remained skeptical of their optimism. I was reminded that the revered black comedian Dick Gregory had once quipped that "a white southern moderate is somebody that will hang you from the low branch of the tree."

Two ministers of the Presbyterian faith—thinking it would showcase their benevolence—invited me to join them for worship at Hattiesburg's First Presbyterian Church. I had walked past the Hardy Street institution many times, musing on how the congregants would react to my black presence. What degree of violence would ensue? Would I be jailed, lynched, or both?

The taller minister placed a hand on my shoulder. A gesture meant to convey resolve: onward Christian soldiers.

"What do you think will happen?" he asked.

I mimed a finger slashing across my throat.

We entered the church and chose a pew. You would have thought I was a purveyor of leprosy; whites scattered like cockroaches leaving us the sole occupants of the pew. The minister nervously officiated.

"This is the Lord's house. Be at peace," he intoned. The less than serene parishioners huddled like praying mantises against the far wall.

"We welcome our guest, but the local boy knows our traditions. His place of worship is across town. Everybody, please stay calm. We will soon resume our regular order of service. The Lord is good," he sermonized.

The prayerful mantises hissed in reply, "The Lord is good. Glory be to the Lord, most high."

I was looking over my shoulder expecting the police to arrive and haul us out. The station was nearby. We decided it was prudent to forgo any further homilies.

Exiting, I was arrested by the police and dumped in the Hattiesburg City Jail.

"Boy, what the fuck do you think you're doing?" The deputy scowled. Silence.

"The church of all places. The house of worship for some of Hattiesburg's finest. I don't know what's come over you people. Got to be all these white northerners down here trying to turn things upside down," he commiserated.

"Get on in there. You better be praying that this don't get out of hand," he admonished, slamming the cell door shut.

The jail cell was small, with a high ceiling, barred window, tiny sink, toilet bowl, and a door slot. My head was abuzz with stories about blacks being disappeared from southern jails. I nervously awaited my fate as earlier childhood memories surfaced. I was comforted by the memory of dad's Sunday afternoon hand-cranked ice creams: the rock salt-packed ice-cold cylinder covered with burlap bagging, and me sitting butt-cold atop, anchoring the wood-encased iron cylinder as dad cranked the handle—wondering if I would live long enough to make more memories. The deputy would occasionally make the rounds.

"You're a lucky nigger, boy. All is quiet outside so far," he chuckled.

It was a nerve-racking sleepless night. I kept jumping up and down trying to spy outside activity through the barred window, sometimes standing on my iron cot, but the barred window was too high.

The morning clanked with the opening of my cell door.

"Well, look at you. You're one lucky coon. The good church minister insisted that he didn't want any bad publicity circulating up north about his church. Get the hell out of here. Your white so-called friends are waiting outside. Your parents better whip some sense into you before some of *us* must," he menaced.

My so-called ministerial friends had retained a New York lawyer. The lawyer later informed me that the charges had been inexplicably dismissed. He surmised that municipal and religious officials did not want the publicity and chose to bury the case.

The ministers, in two days, would drive back to Massachusetts. I was invited along for two weeks to speak on college campuses. Talk about growing up in Hattiesburg and to raise funds for the movement. It was time to talk with dad. Word had not so much spread as seeped into the community concerning my irreligious conduct and arrest. I knew that my actions exposed him and other relatives to potential economic reprisals and physical retaliation.

I told dad of the arrest and the proposed road trip. Dad did not stand in my way. He never spoke of concerns for himself, but of his anxieties for my safety and his wish that I forego the trip.

"It's a good time for me to be out of Hattiesburg," I explained.

"I don't know if this is the best way of doing that. You are smart, Fred, but young and you don't really know nobody up there. Your grandparents will be worried sick. Our family is just trying to hang on. You wouldn't be doing this if your mother was still alive," he bemoaned. His voice cracked and his eyes teared up.

"You might be right about mom. But mom always thought that I would be different. She never really put it into words except calling me her 'little professor,' but this is about you and me. You've done good by me. We're doing more than just hanging on. You've done good," I pleaded.

"You think so?" he asked.

"I know so, dad," I affirmed. "This trip is an opportunity for me to see other regions of the country. To view and experience different ways of seeing. I can't be anybody's 'boy,'" I continued.

"Well, you be careful. There are a lot of false gods out there," he relented.

I was relieved to not be cornered and forced to defy his authority. He had a hard-earned dignity, and I owed him that kernel of respect.

### A Fly in the Buttermilk

Two days later, the three ministers and I started the drive from Hattiesburg to Alabama; Tennessee; Washington, D.C.; Philadelphia; to Northampton, Massachusetts. Integrated travel was a brand new and unsettling occurrence. I was unconvinced that my white companions fully appreciated or anticipated the dangers. Nor did I know what to expect in the northeastern United States. I was amazed at the fully open spaces and cityscapes, the heights of the buildings and the undulating hills and mountains. All seemingly formulaic and unremarkable to my associates.

Crossing Alabama at Birmingham, we exited for lunch at a Howard Johnson Restaurant. I was in no hurry to leave the car. One of the ministers placed his hand on my shoulder and steered me into the restaurant. The service staff, of course, refused to serve an integrated group. Two of the ecclesiastics and I returned to the car. The third ordered take-out service. I watched with some resentment as they ate their fried fish and salad and downed their iced tea. It was a long hungry drive toward Washington, D.C. I refused to eat the racist-tinged food. The three white clergymen must have thought that I was not hungry.

The Washington cold weather revealed my ill-preparedness. We shopped at a Sears Roebucks, the divines paying for my winter clothing choices. We arrived at Northampton in the early evening hours the next day.

Northampton, Massachusetts is a postcard town of adjacent college campuses: Smith College (women), Amherst and Mount Holyoke (co-ed), and the nearby co-ed Springhill campus of the University of Massachusetts.

My host was a Trappist theologian teaching at Smith College. He lived in an off-campus stone monastic dwelling. The house was cold. I longed for the warmth of grandmother's quilts. Meals consisted of bread, cheeses, thick soup, and dark hopped home-brewed beer from the cellar. I nibbled in politeness. My stomach was craving early morning servings of biscuits, grits, and vast slabs of grease-dripping bacon. A young female religion student attended the house. She would be my guide, introducing me to the campuses.

It was eerie having grown up in a cocoon of blackness—now cosseted and interacting with a tsunami of whites. My days consisted of manning information booths: describing Hattiesburg, my childhood, disseminating handouts, explaining voter registration campaigns, and answering questions. Most of the students silently ambled past the booth. I had been brought up to always greet friend, foe, or strangers with a "Morning," or "How y'all doing." This courtesy mostly went unacknowledged! It was akin to being in a foreign country. The language—the cadence was not the same. My speaking tempo was elongated, unhurried, and infused with idiomatic phrases. Their manner of speaking was swift, truncated, and donnish. There was so much I didn't know about their world. I felt faulty, cheated. Most of them knew little or nothing of my world. Did they, too, feel faulty? Cheated? I doubted it.

My evenings were devoted to blanket-swaddled readings of Albert Camus, Jean-Paul Sartre, C. Wright Mills, Paul Tillich, Henry David Thoreau, Paul Goodman, and Bertrand Russell. Books that my campus guide recommended and got from the Frost Library at Amherst College.

My tour was garnering headlines on campus and in local newspapers. I had amassed $15,000 in donations from student associations and local churches. I received an invitation to speak at a church in Willington, Connecticut, and another to address the Young American Socialist League of Students and the W.E.B. Dubois Club on the campus of Yale University. I returned to Massachusetts and spoke at the University of Massachusetts' Springfield campus.

I was unaware that SNCC had a Campus Travelers Bureau and that my newfound celebrity had caught the attention of SNCC Atlanta headquarters. I had no clue I was acting without their consent until a member of the Springfield audience approached and asked to meet. He introduced himself as Mike Thelwell, Professor of African American Studies and SNCC liaison responsible for the New England states.

"Hey, great job. Your visit surprised me. My assignment is to ensure that all speaking engagements and fundraising events are approved and coordinated by the SNCC Speakers Bureau," he proffered.

"I was not aware of that," I apologized.

"Of course, you weren't. No harm done," he soothed. "We are appreciative of your efforts. I have booked your return flight home by way of Atlanta. SNCC Headquarters would like to meet with you and benefit from your report," he summed up.

"Thank you. Nice meeting you." I swallowed.

The plane crawled down the runway, accelerated speed, and began its climb. My bowels were in an uproar. My ears were pounding. My hands tightly gripped the armrest. I furtively glanced out the window and, just as quickly, kept my eyes forward.

"Coffee or tea?" asked the stewardess. "Are you alright sir? First time flying?" she asked.

It was that obvious! The plane started its descent. The pressurized air was hammering in my ears. The aircraft wheels screeched on the runway, momentarily rearing upward like a wild stallion, and came to a halt. I gingerly stepped off the plane. I needed the nearest washroom.

I provided my report to Atlanta SNCC and traveled by bus to Hattiesburg. It was good to be back home. It was especially gratifying to answer dad's questions about what I had experienced and witness his gleeful reaction to the news that I would be returning to school. However, going forward I would be attending more meetings and missing more school and spending less time at home. Mrs. Ella and others were increasingly warning me to be careful.

### Belly of the Whale

*"I have thought that what is needed is the development of people who are interested not in being leaders as much as in developing leadership in others."*

—Ella Baker, SNCC leadership coach and advisor (1963)

The Hattiesburg headquarters for SNCC, the Council of Federated Organizations (COFO), and later the NAACP were housed in a black-owned hotel on Mobile Street.

Sandy Leigh, a black SNCC field secretary, was the Hattiesburg SNCC project director. Leigh was proficient in five languages and had left Yale University to participate in the movement. Sandy looked like James Baldwin. Big-eyed, full-mouthed, broad smile, receding hairline, tuffs of nappy hair, and long, delicately narrow fingers that were always illuminated by the glow and billowing smoke of a Turkish cigarette.

"You hang around here a lot. You just looking or you want to learn?" he asked.

"I'm looking and learning," I retorted.

"Good answer. But the best method of learning is by doing," he instructed. "You ready to do something?" he asked.

"Like what?" I asked.

"See those maps on the wall?" He pointed. "Well, that's a different way of seeing Hattiesburg." He grinned.

There were two gigantic floor-to-ceiling maps showing granular details of Hattiesburg and Palmer Crossing.

"That's your street, your house. This is where we are." He tapped with a pointer stick. "Our job is to knock on every one of those doors. That's the easy part. We need to convince all those scared occupants to join us at the courthouse on Hattiesburg Freedom Day."

"You among the scared?" he asked.

"Not really," I said.

"Well, you ought to be. Fear can be your best friend. Keep it close to you. It's an early warning system that has nothing to do with not doing, but how to do it," he forecasted.

"We need those scared people in each of those houses to lean on each other in a new way. It's called block organizing. A street captain for each street, and this captain is to be chosen by vote. We need a block captain for each neighborhood. Street captains report to block captains and block captains report to us. That's the way we disseminate information and mobilize the community," he explained.

We walked to the other side of the office.

He pointed and described a mimeograph machine. He demonstrated how it worked by writing large block lettering and attaching the stencil onto the ink drum and cranking the handle. The machine whined and spun out a batch of crude flyers, announcing: Hattiesburg Freedom Day.

He removed the used stencil, wiped clean the drum, and scratched another version. "Now you try," he commanded.

I attempted to align the edges of the stencil underneath the guide pins, smoothed away the wrinkles, and whirled the handle. Gooey gobs of black ink splattered against the wall. Sandy and I looked like oil rig workers.

"Well, maybe it's best if I show you how to work the phone bank," he laughed.

I preferred the phone bank and the making of the "One man, One vote" placards.

"There are 'organizers' and then there are 'Organizers,'" boomed Sandy. "The real Organizers know the value of education. There's nothing sadder than the sight of a weary, empty-headed, lost organizer in search of a cause. Stay in school. Your curfew is 9:00 p.m.," he decreed, and walked me home every evening thereafter.

## Fortuity

> *"There are years that ask questions and years that answer."*
>
> —Zora Neale Hurston, *Their Eyes Were Watching God* (1937)

The call went out for SNCC and CORE organizers to converge on Hattiesburg. Sandy was excited to reunite with Bob Moses and the others.

"You should meet with Bob. I will introduce you," he beamed.

"Who is Bob Moses?" I asked.

"Bob is the director of SNCC field operations in Mississippi," he said.

He handed me a written profile. Bob was born in 1935 in Harlem, New York. He graduated from Hamilton College with a B.A. in Philosophy in 1956 and earned a master's degree in mathematics from Harvard University in 1957.

"Remember what I said to you about real organizers and education. Bob is an educated organizer, an organizer of organizers, a facilitator of grassroots and community-based leadership. Now don't get me wrong. Not every educated person can become an organizer," he concluded.

Bob Moses arrived the next day. He was a tallish man with caramel skin, big eyes bedecked with thick lenses, and he was dressed in denim overalls.

I sat nervously hugging the wall—straining to decipher his words—hushed by his subdued manner of speaking. He crossed the room with outstretched hand. I stood and clasped his extended hand.

"Bob," he said. I almost had to lean in to hear his voice.

"Fred," I said at a slightly more audible decibel.

"Sandy thought I should meet with you. Perhaps we can find some time after the rally," he said.

"Welcome to Hattiesburg," I said.

"Tomorrow," he closed.

The following night, two hundred or more packed into St. Paul's Methodist Church. The morning of January 22, 1964, was a cold and rainy day. Nearly 150 people encircled the courthouse, climbed the steps, as others orderly filed into the office of the registrar of voters. Newspapers and television cameras documented the event. Police bullhorns commanded us to disperse, but our line held.

Fannie Lou Hamer kept our spirits high. Mrs. Hamer was short of stature but nevertheless embodied a gigantic and mesmerizing aura. She hobbled with one leg shorter than the other—the result of a police officer beating in Winona, Mississippi. Her skin was dark like sun dried leather. Today, she hoisted a "freedom now" placard, face rain-soaked, flinging her freedom song upwards. "Which side are you on?" The defiant lyrics ricocheted across the rain-sodden courthouse plaza.

Sandy, brooding mother hen, made sure that I marched beside him. Mobile Street black merchants supplied water,

Mrs. Fannie Lou Hamer was short of stature but nevertheless embodied a gigantic and mesmerizing aura.
(Photo courtesy of Matt Heron Photography)

coffee, and food. It had not been a bloodless day: a white Yale Law student, Oscar Chase, was attacked and savagely beaten by a group of white onlookers. Bob was arrested and charged with violation of a city ordinance—walking on the sidewalk!

Later, I sat on the edge of a conversation about plans for a state-wide campaign. There was a sense of urgency to finalize the campaign dubbed "Mississippi Freedom Summer." I overheard Sandy saying Bob would soon leave Hattiesburg for Clarksdale, Mississippi. I was thinking, "What about our meeting?" My head slumped in disappointment.

Sandy walked over, followed by Bob.

"I told Bob about some of the work that you've been doing here and suggested that you should be hired on as SNCC field secretary," he announced. The words lifted my head and spirit. I was giddy with pride, but just as quickly deflated when told that I would be transferred to the SNCC Project in Greenville, Mississippi.

"It's too dangerous for you and your family to continue as an organizer in Hattiesburg. It's your call," said Bob.

I don't know precisely what Sandy and Moses saw in me. Not unlike many would-be organizers before me, his valorization was enough to inspire you to want to emulate him. All of us would be magnetized by his self-effacing style: his approach to building SNCC as an organization of organizers; the leader versus organizer dialectic; his embrace of Albert Camus' dictum that a person is what he does.

Bob accompanied me home. He remained on the porch, and I went in to speak with dad.

"This is dangerous stuff, Fred. Hattiesburg is a cakewalk compared to some of these other counties," he warned. His voice was tinged with a quality of sadness unheard since the death of my mother.

"It's for the safety of family that I should be located elsewhere," I pleaded. I had to go. SNCC was now my North star.

I skunked to the front porch. Bob entered and spoke with dad, assuring him that I would be looked after.

## The Chosen Few

*"Left foot, peg foot, travelin' on…"*

—African American Folk Song,
*Follow the Drinkin' Gourd* (1928)

I was now officially among the band of brothers and sisters. In the circle of trust, so-called because we could depend on each other in dangerous circumstances. Here we were choosing to leave school and be submerged deep down in hazardous, isolated, and rural communities, coalescing with local activists to organize from the bottom-up.

SNCC was uniquely the first full-time professional organizing cadre of the civil rights movement—salaried at $10 per week, or $9.64 after deductions. Workers with families received larger stipends. Our survival depended on black community households who, at significant risk to themselves and their children, provided housing and food. We had to consistently demonstrate our seriousness as organizers to earn their trust and sacrifices—black restaurants offered free meals, barbers cut hair, and doctors tended to medical needs.

I traveled north to Greenville, Mississippi with Bob, Dona Richards, and Lawrence Guyot. Bob, in his characteristically gentle voice, broke down his concept of community organizing, likening it to a troubled boat on the water: all occupants perpetually bailing water to keep afloat. It was the organizers' Sisyphean burden of identifying and nurturing local leadership to get on board.

Nearing Pocahontas, Mississippi, the flashing lights and wailing sirens of state troopers commanded us to pull onto the shoulder of the road.

"I will do the talking," said Bob.

The more elephantine trooper approached.

"Where y'all going," he spat.

Bob is famous for answering questions with a question. The frustrated, florid faced, baton-wielding officer smashed the driver-side headlight, returned to their vehicle, and sped off.

We plowed northward, a one-eyed lightning bug navigating the Mississippi Delta's impenetrable, sullen darkness.

At Greenville I was introduced to the Turners—my host family. A family of twenty. Many of the children were grown and living away. At home were Delores, twenty-something and stunningly beautiful; Edna and Dora, sixteen and seventeen, both equally attractive; and nine-year-old Michael. Mr. Turner, it was clear, had acquiesced to his wife's offer of housing. He had one hammered codicil:

"Don't be messing with my daughters," he exclaimed.

SNCC had already cautioned us to shun romantic relationships with members of host families. Mrs. Turner, a woman of some heft, oversaw an immaculate household. She was also a clandestine smoker and fond of corn whiskey.

Mr. Turner, an electrician by trade, miniature in size, and staunchly religious, was abhorrent of tobacco and alcohol. He was a founding member of a black Gospel quartet and host of a Mississippi delta Gospel radio broadcast. He sang a lilting alto imbued with an emotive timbre. It was a voice and household that soothed my anxieties.

Dona and Bob said their goodbyes. Bob, ever the teacher, gave me a satchel of books: E. Franklin Frazier's *The Black Bourgeoisie*; Albert Camus' *The Myth of Sisyphus and Resistance, Rebellion and Death*; W.E.B. DuBois' *Black Reconstruction in America: An Essay Toward a History of the Part Which Black Folk Played in the Attempt to Reconstruct Democracy in America, 1860-1880*; James W. Silver's *Mississippi: The Closed Society*; Paul Robeson's *Here I Stand*; and Frantz Fanon's *The Wretched of the Earth*.

CHAPTER THREE
# GREENVILLE, MISSISSIPPI
## Queen of the Mississippi Delta

> *"They tried to bury us; they did not know that we were seeds."*
>
> —Dinos Christianopoulos,
> *The Body and the Wormwood* (1960-1993)

Greenville, Mississippi—then with a population of 30,000—is the county seat of Washington County. It is nestled in the territory of historic cotton plantations and the folkways of the Mississippi Delta. It is one of the largest Delta cities, with an unusually diverse population of blacks, whites, Chinese, Creoles, Jews, Italians, and immigrants from Lebanon and Syria. The town was considered by many to be an oasis in the fetid swamplands of Mississippi's racial hostilities. It projected an aura of gentility, cultivated by its coterie of famous artists: Shelby Foote, Ellen Douglass, David Cohen, and the black author William Attaway. As well as leading businessmen, such as the Harding Carter family who owned and published the Pulitzer Prize-winning *Delta Democrat-Times*. It had a small detachment of Negro policemen assigned primarily to patrol the black community and disempowered to arrest whites.

However true, this fool's gold veneering did not preclude a segregated caste structure and daily assaults upon the dignity of Greenville's black residents.

In stark contrast were the adjacent, racially intransigent bellicose towns and hamlets of Leland, Hollandale, Metcalfe, Arcola, Bellewood, Glen Allan, Winterville, Avon, Wayside, Isola, and the abutting Sharkey and Issaquena counties. These anomalies can only be fully understood through the prism of the cultural anthropology of the delta. This vast alluvial plain gave birth to the blues. Where cotton was king, and the descendants of slaves still outnumber their former masters. This was where the sharecropping labor system and other vestiges of slavery were most real. All made worse by droughts, floods, and infestations of the cotton bud-eating boll weevil. Here, mechanization of cotton production had rendered superfluous its vast ranks of poor black laborers. Legendary bluesman Charlie Patton sang of this beetle-like insect in his *Mississippi Bo Weevil Blues*:

> "Sees a little boll weevil keeps movin' in the...Lordy!
> You can plant your cotton, and you won't get a half a bale, Lordy
> Boll weevil, bo weevil, where's your native home? Lordy
> 'A-Louisiana raised in Texas,
> Least is where I was bred and born,' Lordy..." (1929)

Wandering has been a favored thread in blues verses, and highways have always epitomized the possibility of laying down tracks to higher and better grounds. Laying my burdens down or seeking renewal elsewhere.

Highway 61, now historically designated the Mississippi Blues Trail, is the redolent northward conduit out of Mississippi. Beginning in downtown New Orleans and looping Baton Rouge; meandering Mississippi by way of Natchez, Vicksburg, Leland, Cleveland, Clarksdale, and Tunica; circling Memphis and northward to the Canadian border. The

Highway 61 alumni of Mississippi bluesmen include B.B. King, Robert Johnson, Charley Patton, Muddy Waters, Howlin' Wolf, Sonny Boy Williamson, Ike Turner, Sam Cooke, James Cotton, Jimmy Reed, Junior Parker, and Willie Love. These itinerant blues tricksters while moaning tunes of agitation and melancholy, spinning tall tales and real stories of African American resistance, double entendre twelve-stringed, bottle-necked-cloaked blueprints about how to speak to the "boss man" and yet hold fast to dignity.

Greenville's Nelson Street is the core of the black business district. Home to nightclubs—such as the Casablanca, Flowing Fountain, and Silver Dollar Cafe—and churches, groceries, fish markets, May's and Bailey's restaurants, barbershops, laundries, record shops, and a multitude of other enterprises. Legendary bluesman Willie Love immortalized this stop on the blues trail in his 1951 recording "Nelson Street Blues":

"I'm all dressed up now from my,
head to my shoes.
Now sit back and relax, whilst I play these Nelson Street Blues..."

The Greenville SNCC office was housed on the third floor of the black-owned Nelson Street Carter Building. I entered the small office, furnished with a desk, Remington typewriter, telephone, filing cabinet, a binder of contact information, and a wall map of the state of Mississippi. Greenville, Washington, and other surrounding hamlets were underlined in red.

I began reading the field notes of Charlie Cobb. Charlie, a black Howard University student, had been assigned as Project Director for Greenville in the summer of 1963. He had cultivated contacts and organized a student union at the black Greenville High School.

Muriel Tillinghast, another black Howard University student, was now directing the Washington, Issaquena, and

Sharkey County Project. I would soon discover that she was an afro bandana-headed, exceptionally bright woman with a straight-arrow personality and immense knowledge of her territory's geography and demographics. She was now delayed in Greenwood, Mississippi.

The phone rang. It was Muriel.

"Welcome to Greenville, Fred," she said.

"Thank you, Muriel. Looking forward to meeting you," I responded.

"Lots of work to be done. We can use all the man and woman power that we can get. We will soon be a staff of twelve. Counting you, Charlie, Jesse Davis, and myself," she envisioned.

"That's a good start. Charlie and Jesse are good people."

"And you!" I quickly added.

## Antebellum Blues

The next morning, after a full office day, Dolores Turner provided a driving tour of Greenville's outlying regions.

In Wayside, Mississippi stood the Belmont Plantation Mansion. The pamphlet described a 9,000-square-foot antebellum behemoth of a plantation established in 1857. It was liberated in 1863 by Union Army forces. It was now a wedding and events space, bed and breakfast, public attraction, and corporate retreat venue.

This was, for me, a ghostly *Gone with the Wind* moment. Nothing in this modern iteration was suggestive of shackles, whips, branding irons, auction blocks, separated families, or countless bones calcifying in unmarked graves. The scene was a farcical, reductive, revisionist, whitened, antiseptic historical narrative. A 'now you see me, now you don't' parody that called to mind the words of American writer and critic Edmund Wilson, that "the North had won the war, but the South had won the literature." I decided to go inside. There was a white-gloved black doorman. One can only surmise, being generous, that his presence was yet another unintended parody. The two of us, nonetheless, shared a code-switching instance signifying "What the hell are we doing here?"

Leaving, a phalanx of white tourists entered with not a single black amongst them. The doorman nodded knowingly in my direction. There was no exchange of words; only such gestures could telegraph our shared history.

Muriel, days later, convened a staff meeting to assess project needs and staff allocation. John Sawyer would be responsible for communications. Charlie Cobb would assist her in directorial responsibilities. The soon-to-be white volunteers would organize in the relatively safe environs of Greenville.

"Fred and Jesse Davis will be the advance team for community insertion and organizing in Issaquena and Sharkey Counties," said Muriel.

### Out on a Limb

*"Being Poor Is Expensive."*

—James Baldwin, *Nobody Knows My Name* (1961)

End of the week plans were in place for my travel to Mayersville, Mississippi. The county seat of Issaquena County—population of 1,635. Mayersville is a small Mississippi River town of 300 nuzzled against the high-mounded levee. Blacks, in 1964, composed 68 percent of the population. One hundred percent of the whites were registered voters. But not a single black resident. Black neighborhoods had no running water, paved streets, or sewers, and were without electricity.

The 42-mile drive was timed for arrival in darkness. SNCC now had a fleet of dependable, fast, CB radio-equipped vehicles with aerial antennas mounted on the rear. KUY-1106 was our call sequence, squawking locations or messages of distress. This nevertheless failed to assuage my anxieties as these assigned vehicles were eponymously tagged, The Sojourner Truth Fleet, in honor of the famed black abolitionist and were recognizable state-wide by police and local Klan chapters. My sleeping bag was at the ready, my haversack packed with a water canteen, canned sardines, saltine crackers, compass, toothpaste, brush, facial cloth, soap, hand lotion, cigarettes, matches, pocketknife, pens, and notepads.

Local SNCC volunteer Willie Rollins would be my designated wheelman. His selection would soon become apparent. He was a tall, slender, highly strung, gum-chewing, chain smoker of few words but imbued with a cagey comprehension of the main highways, backroads, pathways, alleyways, logging, and cow trails. He could dim, cut lights, and deftly navigate fields of cotton or sugar cane. His periscope swiveling neck would continuously gyroscope from rear-view to side mirrors.

Unita Blackwell would be my host and the owner of the town's few telephones. She was Amazonian in height and of what we referred to as jet blue-black hue. She possessed the most incandescent eyes and shoulder length woolly hair. Her voice was robust but sugarcane sweet. She grew up in a sharecropping family that eked out a meager living in the harsh sharecropping and cotton-picking economy. Married, thirty-two years of age, she, her husband, and seven-year-old son lived in a shotgun cabin, at some distance from neighbors. The husband, John, would sometimes be away for days at his job on the levee.

I had been told that Mrs. Blackwell had previously befriended SNCC organizers Charlie Cobb and Ivanhoe Donaldson in 1963, when the two were forced at gunpoint to flee neighboring Sharkey County. She signed on as an

Nothing had prepared the author for this granular underbelly of impoverishment. (Photos courtesy of Herschel Kaminsky)

SNCC organizer in 1964 and would soon become a leading figure in the Mississippi Freedom Democratic Party. Years later, in 1969, she would be elected the first black mayor of Mayersville. Serving twenty-five years, she would bring electricity, streetlights, running water, sewers, and paved streets to the black districts.

Willie dropped me off and drove away. Only Unita Blackwell and a few trusted neighbors were to know my identity and purpose. All others would know me as her visiting nephew from Tchula, Mississippi. Mrs. Blackwell had arranged my lodging with widower Roy Williamson and his young son.

The next morning over breakfast we discussed the challenges and our personal safety plans and reviewed her list of likely voter registration recruits.

"Canvassing will be difficult, Fred. Housing is remote and scattered. All the roads are nearly inaccessible except by pick-up truck, tractor, horse, or muleback. My neighbor has a stubborn but gentle mule. Just know that the plantation owners are empowered to shoot trespassers on sight," warned Unita.

I had visions of my gun-riddled sixteen-year-old corpse oozing blood, bedewing, and saturating the whiteness of the cotton. Too young to die. Too young for such a mission. Did I know what I was getting into? Yes and no. I had some idea what was expected of me. But was I too young to be trusted with such a mission? This was, after all, my first solo mission. I would have to trust my training and improvise within the circumstances. I traveled mostly on mule-back, tethering the animal in the brush and walking the clearing to the first visible galvanized tin-roofed shanty-house.

I had read SNCC's briefing documents on black poverty and hunger in the Mississippi Delta. But nothing had prepared me for this granular underbelly of impoverishment: the shacks with tar-paper or cardboard walls; open slatted flooring; paneless windows; leaking roofs; and children, children, children. Big-eyed, running noses, coughing, open sores, and distended bellies atop spindly legs. The mother breastfed the youngest, avoiding my gaze, anticipating unasked questions.

"The children's sores are from rat bites," she volunteered.

The county, according to the Mississippi Bureau of Family Statistics, is infamous for its high rate of black infant mortality, even by Mississippi standards. The shack was sparsely furnished: corn-shuck mattresses, chamber pots, and the drone of swarming flies. One large bedroom, a small kitchen, and a lopsided front porch.

Days of canvassing unspooled an endless selfsame vista of hungry toddlers, dilapidated shanties, and dejected weary-eyed mothers. There was, in my nightly field notes, a tension. A tussle for the precise nomenclature which had condemned these children to the fourth circle of Dante's Inferno. It was clear that I needed to go slow. Do no harm. Handle with care the fragility of these lives. Going forward, I would ask for and expect little or nothing—simply becoming an abiding face of comfort—often sitting on front porches and sharing my lunch with children.

After weeks of canvassing, Unita and I discussed the way forward over a late-night supper. It was evident that we were both weighing the poundage of our individual and collective calculus of putting impoverished, powerless people in harm's way. It was unlikely that we could muster enough community support for a courthouse voter registration turnout. Failure to do so would further increase their sense of fear and paralysis. We decided, instead, to pivot away from a strategy of mobilization and focus on mass education.

## Ballots or Bullets

> *"People hear whispers as loud as guns"*
>
> —Elizabeth Spencer, *Voices at the Back Door* (1956)

In the late-night hours, we were jolted from sleep by sounds of breaking shards of glass. I recognized from my hunting days the familiar recoiling, staccato, bolt-action of long-arm rifles. I grabbed the Williamson son and pulled him underneath the bed and recognized the thudding sound of Mr. Williamson doing the same in the nearby bedroom. We lay silently on the floorboards for what seemed like hours. Thirty minutes later we were hugging and assuring each other that all were uninjured. The boy's body was convulsed with tremors and his eyes bulged with fear. I was air-hungered, wheezing, and gasping for breath. I had known fear in my young life, but this was poles apart from anything previously experienced. This was ghoulish dread. Stomach-churning terror. It was clear that the three of us were no longer safe on the property.

Unita and John heard the cracking and rushed over.

"It's Fred that's in danger. They are trying to scare him off and send a message to the rest of us. We need to quickly move him elsewhere," she added.

She readied a food box of cornbread, baked beans, collard greens, catfish, and a jug of water. Soon a horse-drawn wagon pulled up to the cabin. It was Mr. Edwards—a local dairy farmer—and his teenage son.

I crawled into the wagon bed and was secreted beneath a piling of feed sacks, corn shucking's, and housed in the hayloft of his backyard barn. It was a warm but restless sleep amongst the mooing cows and the wafting aroma of the chloric acids of urine and liquid manure gases. The night was noisy with the raspy callings of bullfrogs and the hissings of crickets. My anxieties gradually succumbed to twitchy, chary sleep.

In the morning, I accompanied Unita and John to report the gunfire to Sheriff J.A. Darnell. He was, as expected, dismissive.

"This was all likely a dispute between neighbors. It might even have been the work of —pointing at me—'your so-called nephew.' I might end up having to arrest him," he threatened.

### Unlock Me, Lord

> *"Remember the day, I remember it well*
> *My dungeon shook and my chain fail off"*
>
> —Negro Spiritual, *I Am Free* (10-11)

In the afternoon I continued my round of visiting families. Unita continued to bravely open her local store. The two of us agreed that it was vital that we be seen as undeterred.

Passing Greenbriar Cemetery, family plot of the nineteenth-century plantation owners, I was arrested and placed in the Issaquena County Jail. My watch, money, and belt were removed. However, I was still in possession of pen and paper, secreted in the band of my sock. During the night, a jail trustee tossed a chamber pot of piss into the cell and deprived me of sleep by late-night banging of nightsticks on my cell bars and endless rounds of flashlight beaming, racial insults, and threats of how easily I could be made to disappear. I felt emotionally stretched and nauseous, bilious fluids secreting underneath my tongue, bowels tense and clamoring.

I was experiencing a skewed sense of time. I tried to self-regulate my emotions by humming familiar tunes, breathing exercises, and pacing the cell floor on timorous legs and counting my steps. A trustee discovered me scribbling notes and insisted that I surrender my paper and pen. I shredded my notes and gave up the pen. He angrily kicked my legs from under me, spat on me, and punched me in the right side of my head. Later, at mealtime, he opened the cell door and hurled the plate of food and hot coffee. The hot coffee narrowly missed, with the cup shattering into shards against the bars. The food plate was a bull's eye hit to my chest, the gooey, congealed concoction sliding down my pant legs.

I dulled the ache of passing time by attempting to reassemble the puzzle of my tattered jottings. I was uncertain as to how long my ordeal would last and feared the worst was yet to come but remained confident that Unita had informed Greenville of my incarceration.

Two days later, a black Greenville lawyer arranged for my release. The noonday sun shone brightly. My teary eyes stung adjusting to the glare as Unita and John supported my wobbly walk to the truck.

Two evenings later we were scheduled to meet at Moon Lake Church. I met with Unita to discuss the way forward. We understood the need to lower expectations; my jailing and the previous gunfire incident had ratcheted up fear, and people were now even more reluctant at voter registration efforts.

The church gathering, by quick count, was fifteen sharecroppers. Unita approached the podium and started a doleful yet assertive humming, which was lifted into song by the congregants:
"Oh, freedom
Oh, freedom over me
And before I'd be a slave
I'd be buried in my grave
And go home to my Lord and be free
Oh, freedom."

### If Not Action, Then Intent

"We are on the long walk home. Some of you will have to crawl before you walk. Sometimes it will be one step forwards and two steps backwards. But we will get there someday. To make a small town achieve its potential you need everybody. When a crippled person carries a blind person, who can't see, both get to where they're going," Unita told them. I spoke a few words of gratitude for their generosity and protection.

"Tomorrow will not be long in coming, and SNCC will return in a few months," I promised.

There was a smattering of "amens," and some hugs and tears. Unita and I waved goodbye to the silhouettes melding into the darkness.

In the morning, I took the small Mayersville's roadside bus to Rolling Fork, Mississippi—the county seat of neighboring Sharkey County. The town of Rolling Fork is famous for being the birthplace of blues legend McKinley Morganfield, aka Muddy Waters. I was there to meet with the chairman of the local NAACP chapter. His report on the towns of Rolling Fork and Anguilla mirrored the mood and conditions in Issaquena County. Over lunch we discussed how to increase collaboration between the neighboring counties.

He drove me back to Unita's. She cooked and spoke of our experiences and her hopes for her small town and county. She was proud and convinced that our tiny nucleus of supporters would stay the course; that our conduct had set an example, word would spread, and others would eventually come aboard. I silently agreed. That was the long view, but I was embroiled in the short view. Did I move too fast? Exposing myself and others to danger? What could or should I do differently on my next assignment?

Unita placed a hand on my shoulder as if hearing my inner dialogue.

"No ifs," she said.

## On the Road from Damascus

A car pulled up after supper and flashed its lights. Willie was there, by prearrangement, to drive me back to Greenville. I said my goodbyes to Unita, John, and the son.

Willie nodded and spoke the call number, KUY-1106, into the handheld CB radio, "Highway 1, Greenville bound." He was otherwise silent as ever, momentarily resting a hand on my knee and proffering one of his stringent Lucky Strike cigarettes. I sat wordlessly in the blue night of the delta, the roads intermittently illuminated by fireflies circling in and out of the brooding shadows of the ubiquitous Sycamore and Magnolia trees. My nostrils dilated under the anesthesia of the cloying smells of honeysuckle. I remained in a dark mood, blinded by what-ifs and buts and searching for the higher ground of "was blind, but now I see," clutching the belief that we were cultivating hardiness zones, seeding furrows of resistance soon to burst into blooms of local leadership.

Willie drove the back roads, only intersecting Highway 1 at Greenville, and pulled in for a beer at May's Restaurant Bar and Grill. Willie downed his Schlitz beer and enunciated the longest sentence that I would ever hear him speak: "Boy, you are crazy. I heard about the gun fire. I kept asking if it was time to get you outta there only to be told that you would contact the office and say when."

Back at the SNCC office, I called dad to check up on the family. I assured him, omitting details about the shooting and arrest, that I was well. It was reassuring to hear his surprised and undulating-stuttered call of my name.

"Thank God you're still okay," he said.

I visualized him rocking gently in his cane-bottomed chair, black coffee pouring to saucer, the harmonious slurp and sipping—an evocative gesture of warmth and absence. I missed him.

"I love you, dad," I said tearfully. A solicitude never directly expressed in our household.

"Be strong, boy," he replied.

I called my grandparents. After many rings my grandmother answered and immediately began crying.

"We are worried, sick. Come home," she pleaded.

"I am doing okay, grandma, and will soon come to visit you," I assured.

"That's not what I meant," she hissed into the phone.

"I know," I said.

"Grandma, dad is just as worried and concerned as you are. He did not want me to leave home and did his best to convince me not to leave. I am coming to see you very soon."

I asked to speak with my grandfather.

"I don't think that's a good notion," she said.

Grandfather took the phone.

"I hope it's true that you are coming for a visit. I told your grandmother to stop badmouthing your dad. That it was just as likely my fault for putting you up on that mule wagon alongside me, driving the backroads delivering supplies to the poor. Too much for young eyes to see. Not to mention the killing of your cousin Sammy. I am waiting for your visit. I will say your goodbyes to your grandmother."

I rejoined Willie for the drive to the Turners'. The Sidney Street house was in darkness. I sat on the front porch steps decompressing and being grateful that I was back in the bosom of relative safety.

The house was suddenly ablaze with lights and laughter. The Turners were standing in the doorway and shouting for me to come inside. The kitchen table was a cornucopia of chicken, pork chops, fish, collard greens, black-eyed peas, rice, macaroni, and cheese, iced tea, and buttermilk. It was a meal befitting a prodigal son. Mr. Turner was away on the gospel circuit. Mrs. Turner and I sat on the front porch, smoked cigarettes, and drank from her jar of corn whiskey. She asked and I told until my eyelids were too heavy with exhaustion. I went to bed for a fitful sleep disturbed by body tremors, low grade fever, and sweats. The following evening, semi-awake, I heard her speak into the phone that I was clubbing on Nelson Street with Delores. I admired her diversionary mendacity but wondered what Delores' boyfriend would have thought of such an outing. She later informed me that I needed to return a call to Ella Gaston from Hattiesburg.

It felt good to be off the highway and backroads and sleeping in a bed instead of the barn loft's scratchy hay and openness to the unknown perils of the delta darkness.

Days later, I boarded the early morning greyhound bus to Hattiesburg. I steered clear of the 326 Lee Street front entrance and walked the back laneway to the rear entrance. I saw dad hoeing furrows and dropping seeds in his backyard garden. He heard the unhitching of the gate lock, dropped the hoe, wiped the sweat from his eyes, smiled and shook his head.

"You are a God welcome ghost, a sight for sore eyes. How long you are staying?" he asked. "Just a few hours. I need to get back to Greenville. Early morning plans," I lied. I left unsaid my safety concerns for me, him, and family if I stayed overnight in Hattiesburg. I needed to be out of town before the witching hour. "Well come on in the house. You hungry?" he asked. Anticipating a no answer, he laid the table with biscuits, jam, a hefty slice of his homemade pound cake and brewed coffee. We sat in his signature rocking chairs, with cane seat and back, husking oven-roasted peanuts and slowly sipping the chicory black infused coffee.

"The sun is getting high dad. Let me help you finish the furrowing and seeding," I offered. "You sure?" he asked. I hoed and he dropped seeds until the Mississippi sun beat down and heat rose from the soil. Later, he poured crushed walnut, and a whiskey-soaked raisin-scented elixir into a cylinder encased in ice, rock salt, and overlaid with burlap. I cranked the handle, and we scooped ice-cream underneath the chinaberry tree.

"Well dad, I must get going and see my grandparents, Aunt Lula, Ella Gaston, and a few friends. I will keep in touch." He extended his hand. "Thanks for the visit. I worry about you." "I will be alright." I bravely assured. He knew. I knew. We knew as SNCC workers that all such goodbyes could be the last time. Neighbors waved from front porches as I walked to 116 Lee Street. My door knocking was not answered. I walked to the kitchen and saw grandmother stringing laundry on the backyard clothesline. The whiter than ever bed sheets billowed and swayed like kites in the breeze.

"Hello grandma," I greeted. She looked up. Clothespins clenched in teeth. Dropped the hamper, gripped her walking cane, and hobbled into the kitchen. She nodded for me to be seated. Washed her hands and gently massaged my head. I watched as she opened the fridge, poured iced tea, and served me a bowl of peach cobbler. I knew with certainty, as surely as her God knew, that she would not utter a word before this venerable ritual had been honored.

"Your grandfather is out and about. You don't look too bad. Somebody must be feeding you," she observed. "You are not looking bad yourself," I complimented. We moved to the parlor, and she pulled the rocking chair near the quilting frame. I sat across and threaded needles. The listening post of my childhood. I could clearly see the emergent railroad cross-themed quilt. I surveyed the walls lined with rolls of cotton batting, the many layered drawers of scissors, pinking shears, variegated colors of threads, curved pins, rulers, clips, hoops, ironing board, and the basket of scrap fabrics. The stations of her cross. Her redemptive garden of reordered chaos. "I remember that you loved being in this room and how your eyes would shine, and ears perk up as we told stories of yesterday and dreams of tomorrow," she wistfully recalled. "I will never forget. Those were some hard-earned stories. Sometimes enraging, tinged with sadness, and difficult listening. But there was always the drumbeating message that we must keep on keeping on. It was the best of all your gifts," I told her. "We can always thank the Lord for wisdom and small things. Like bringing you safely back home. I know that you have chosen your path, and this is only a visit. So, you get no further pleadings. Only my prayers," she conceded. "Your prayers are no small thing," I assured her. "I know that you are anxious to see others, but you will, before leaving town, come by to see your grandfather," she quizzed. I promised to do so.

Mrs. Ella Gaston skipped down the front steps. Beaming smile. Arms wide open. "Look at you boy. Come on in the house." She served a bowl of rice pudding and a glass of ice-cold water. "Now let's talk. What have you been up to?" she asked. I was effusive about the Turner family, the gun fire incident, the arrest/jail and hideaway in the hayloft, the obscene poverty, the pitiless and incorrigible bigotry, and the indomitable grit of Mississippi Delta black people. "How are you feeling about all that? Were you scared?" she asked. "Yes mam. I was scared. All the time," I offered. This was my first instance of vocally externalizing fears about what I was doing and more, gut wrenchingly, what I was asking others to do. "Good. Don't be a turkey, gobbling and strutting around the boiling pot. Always know where the backdoor is and the cracks in the floorboards. Always be small but big in the moment. I know you know what I mean. I will always be here. Just a phone call away. Now go. I know you have others to see." She kissed my forehead, and I was out the door.

Regrettably, I did not have time to visit Aunt Lula, grandfather, or others. The witching hour, sundown, was fast approaching and I needed to show my backside to Hattiesburg.

# PART II

## CHAPTER FOUR
# MISSISSIPPI FREEDOM SUMMER

> *"...and it was out of those heated discussions that we reached a very uneasy...but at least tentative agreement among most staff, to go ahead with concrete, specific programs."*
>
> —Bob Moses, *Speech on Mississippi Freedom Summer Program*, Stanford University (1964)

> *"Alabama's gotten me so upset*
> *Tennessee made me lose my rest*
> *And everybody knows about Mississippi goddam*
> *...Hound dogs on my trail*
> *School children sitting in jail*
> *Black cat crossed my path*
> *I think every day's gonna be my last..."*
>
> —Nina Simone, *Mississippi Goddam* (1964)

It was a summer of mass arrests, arson, beatings, evictions, firings, murder, spying, and other forms of intimidation and harassment: a ten-week fast-moving summer storm with high and gusting winds of hate. At least three Mississippi blacks were murdered because they supported the civil rights movement.

4 people were critically wounded.

3 civil rights workers were killed.

30 black homes and businesses were bombed or burned.
37 black churches were destroyed or burned.
80 Freedom Summer workers were beaten.
1,062 were arrested.

## Asking the Right Questions

> *"One Scotch, One Bourbon, One Beer."*
>
> —John Lee Hooker, bluesman.
> Tutwiler, Mississippi (1966)

Bob Moses asked to meet over a beer to discuss our disagreements. Though only sixteen years of age, I was painfully aware that I had stood in opposition to my mentor: a personage considered by many to be untouchable and, even then, viewed as an icon in SNCC and the civil rights movement, and the chief architect of the proposed Mississippi Freedom Summer Project.

I and others had outright disagreed with Bob's decision to enroll white student volunteers to assist the Freedom Summer campaign to register the black vote. This was the occasion of the four-day SNCC staff meeting held in Greenville, Mississippi (November 11, 1963). However, I felt confident in my southern roots, and my knowledge of black Mississippians and their complex, tortured history of resistance and struggle against being overpowered by the white presence.

Bob sat in his characteristic pose of calmness.

"It's not that I don't understand and share some of your and others' concerns. But we need to ramp up. We need to shine a brighter light on the closed society of Mississippi. The participation of white volunteers will accomplish that and accelerate the pace of change. The scope of the Summer Project is huge. We need foot soldiers. The size and complexity of this undertaking requires that everybody remains on track," he pleaded.

"Look, Bob. You ran a good meeting. There were some expressed disagreements. All were afforded a fulsome hearing. There were no autocratic shutdowns. Yours and the majority approach prevailed. I will not, going forward, be openly voicing my opposition," I assured.

We embraced, shook hands. I put several coins in the jukebox and punched in several blues tunes. We listened. Drank our beers. Sometimes joining other patrons on the sawdust-strewn dance floor. We left, arms around each other's shoulders, and walked to our sleeping quarters.

Many were concerned about how the disagreement would impact the relationship between the two of us. However, Bob would continue to demonstrate his confidence in me. He continued to see something in me, the tiny flame of my struggle. Which I had not quite divined and had not yet grown into. His confidence ceded me the status of a low-hanging leaf on the decision tree—a perch from which to view central moments and grow into my new and outsized status. I also knew that there would be an end-of-summer critical review of what I, and a few others, considered as the possible unintended organizational consequences of the influx of white volunteers.

The 1964 Mississippi Freedom Summer Campaign was the best and worst of times for the civil rights movement—an inflection point encapsulating SNCC's meteoric rise and fall. At its inception, the summer project was a controversial initiative designed to crack the iceberg of white resistance to black voter registration and pierce the paralysis of fear bulwarked by the state's apparatus of terrorism. By 1964, students and others had already begun integrating public accommodations, registering adults to vote, and, above all, strengthening a network of local leadership. It had been a protracted and deadly struggle that largely failed in registering significant numbers of black voters.

Cresting on the waves of 1963 (including the Freedom Ballot and Freedom Day registration efforts in Greenwood and Hattiesburg), Bob prevailed over the doubts of SNCC and COFO workers regarding his strategy of recruiting and deploying 300-plus white college and university volunteers. I, and several other critical voices, remained doubtful. The actual deployment would exceed one thousand. Bob reckoned that the national media and the nation would care more about white volunteer participation and their well-being. It was hoped that this national concern would potentially restrain violence and brutality against the white volunteers, local blacks, and SNCC activists. The valuing of white lives would put Mississippi's white resistance, the plight of blacks, and SNCC resistance on the national agenda as well. Volunteers were also needed to do the increased footwork necessary to organize the Mississippi Freedom Democratic Party, staff Freedom Schools and Freedom libraries, and farming and quilting cooperatives.

Our opposition to this idea centered on the pride and value we gave to the legacy of SNCC as a southern-bred and black-led insurgency. We feared that this influx of white volunteers would fundamentally alter our leadership, organizational structure, and organizing tradition as recounted in Charles M. Payne's, *I've Got the Light of Freedom: The Organizing Tradition of the Mississippi Freedom Struggle*. We were also worried that the white volunteers would be leaving at summer's end, and so would the national media—resulting in local black Mississippians and SNCC organizers suffering the venom of unrestrained white rage. It was, ultimately, the weight of the opinion of Fannie Lou Hamer and other seasoned local black leaders that tipped the scale in favor of white volunteers. The Mississippi Summer Project, for them, represented a hinge moment—a juncture, period or age when the movement could go in one direction or another with a

David Bernstein interviews Fred Anderson for film about Fannie Lou Hamer by Alice J. Bernstein, Montreal, August 27, 2006. (Photo by Rachel J. Bernstein)

starkly different outcome. They reasoned that if white volunteers or anybody willing to risk their lives to seize the moment were needed, they should be welcomed. Message received.

Bob's strategy, in the short-term, was correct. I think our concerns, in the long-term, were proven right, resulting in deleterious impacts on the future of SNCC. This was the first vocal policy disagreement between Bob and me, and the reason that prompted our beer meeting.

## Uncommon Knowledge

I, along with others in the opposition, had also been born and bred in the local briar patch. We felt that we better understood how the power dynamics and interactions nurtured a racialized dependency and tendencies of Mississippi blacks to defer to the white presence and intrusion.

The need and right to self-defence also ended in another heated disagreement. SNCC had always adhered to Gandhi and Martin Luther King's philosophy of nonviolence. However, many of us adopted nonviolence as a strategic umbrella rather than a fixed philosophy. Many SNCC organizers, including myself, were frequently armed. We had no intention of turning the other cheek, being brutalized, and murdered as we drove the unlit backroads of Mississippi. Black sharecroppers, farmers, and other local blacks were frequently armed and determined to defend their property and families. These were the people who provided us—at considerable risk to self and family—housing and refuge.

We knew the first-hand account of Hartman Turnbow—black farmer and grandson of slaves residing in Mileston, Mississippi. He had returned fire, hitting one in a group of white bandits attempting to firebomb his home. He had been arrested and charged with trying to firebomb his own house! Bob Moses, who was housed there at the time, was also incarcerated. Once, when Mr. Turnbow provided Jesse Davis and me with lodging, he immediately pointed out the location of his arsenal. It was clear that, if need be, we were expected to join in the defense of his home.

"This nonviolent stuff'll get you killed," he told every lodger as referenced in Charlie Cobbs' *This Nonviolent Stuff'll Get You Killed: How Guns Made Civil Rights Possible*.

We felt duty-bound to join him and others in their resolve to protect their homes and families against the assault of marauding white mobs. The debate, for us, was critical. Bob and others had assured the U.S. Justice Department, donors, and white parents that the campaign's sole focus would be confined to black voter registration efforts. There were to be no public demonstrations or direct actions that would increase danger to the volunteers. There was also the express fear that any public notice of SNCC organizers being arrested on charges of bearing arms would jeopardize the project. Bob's internal compromise was that local blacks had the right to be armed for the sake of self-defence of property and family.

They were, ironically, already so empowered. They had exercised and would continue to exercise their second amendment right with or without our approval, while those of us in the opposition would, with or without organizational consent, assist in that tradition. Akinyele Umoja provides a fulsome narrative of this legacy in *We Will Shoot Back: Armed Resistance in the Mississippi Freedom Movement*.

The recruitment campaign netted more than one thousand out-of-state volunteers. Two one-week orientation sessions for the volunteers were held at Western College for Women in Oxford, Ohio (now part of Miami University), from June 13 to 20, and June 21 to 28, 1964. SNCC organizers would educate volunteers on the history of Mississippi, the freedom movement, area assignments, nonviolent practices, and the Mississippi Freedom Summer Project's goals and strategies. I was excited in anticipation of renewing acquaintances with my band of brothers and sisters from across Mississippi.

### Driving While Black

> *"Ain't gon' let nobody turn me around."*
> —SNCC Freedom Singers (1962)

Cynthia Washington, the SNCC Project Director of Bolivar County, Mississippi, and I started on the drive for Oxford, Ohio. Cynthia was a twenty-three-year-old, no-nonsense woman, an agile driver, courageous, and always armed. We traveled the Mississippi Delta northward towards Memphis, Tennessee, until flashing red lights and a howling siren pulled us over at Knoxville, Tennessee.

Cynthia handed her 38-caliber pistol to me. I concealed the gun beneath the front floorboard of the vehicle.

The taller of the deputy sheriffs announced, "Y'all ain't going to no civil rights gathering today. Y'all ain't gon' be bringing those white northerners down here to stir up trouble." He scowled. The other deputy climbed into our car.

We were escorted and booked into the Knoxville County Jail.

We were released in the early morning and told to find our way back to Mississippi. Cynthia and I were relieved that the car had not been searched.

Cynthia looped through the lower-lying regions of Arkansas, avoiding Knoxville, and exiting at Memphis, bound for Oxford, Ohio. We finally arrived on the morning of June 11. Two days before the volunteers.

We were greeted by Bob Moses, John Lewis (SNCC chairman), Julian Bond (Communications Director), James Forman (Executive Director), Ruby Doris Smith-Robinson (Administrator, Atlanta Office), and Ella Baker (SNCC Founder/Advisor). There were loud shouts of greetings from SNCC organizers hunkered down in the shade of campus trees. All were busy in discussions and reviewing their orientation notebooks. Ruby Doris showed the two of us the layout of campus facilities and led us to the Elliott and Stoddard Hall dormitories. We were all to assemble later in Peabody Hall. I devoted some time to unpacking, organizing my room, and making calls to dad and grandparents.

I joined the others for a plenary session and dinner in the Harrison Hall Cafeteria. The kitchen was staffed by a paid coterie of black cooks from Mississippi. Ruby Doris Smith, leaving nothing to chance, had ensured that we were well fed, and that the white volunteers would be introduced to Mississippi's black cuisine.

The hall was boisterous. We table-hopped and renewed acquaintances. The lights dimmed. The SNCC Freedom Singers stood center stage. They lifted a song that captured the longing and the spirit of our organizing tradition, our beloved community:

> *"They say that freedom is a constant struggle…*
> *Oh Lord, We struggled so long*
> *We must be free, we must be free*
> *They say that freedom is a constant crying…*
> *Oh Lord, we've cried so long*
> *We must be free, we must be free…*
> *They say that freedom is a constant sorrow…*
> *Oh, Lord, we've sorrowed so long*
> *We must be free, we must be free*
> *They say that freedom is a constant moaning…*
> *Oh Lord, we've been moaning so long*
> *We must be free, we must be free*
> *They say that freedom is a constant dying…*
> *Oh Lord, we've been dying so long*
> *We must be free, we must be free."*

It was a moment of grounding. Some heads were bowed. All eyes were wet. All consoled each other. All arose in applause, not unlike the frictional heat of a match bursting into flame.

Bob now stood at the microphone. "The overarching aim of Mississippi Freedom Summer," he explained, "is to create a political crisis. Only when metal has been brought to white heat can it be shaped and molded. And so, it must be with Mississippi's iceberg of racism and exploitation," he encouraged.

The Summer Project would consist of four activities: voter registration and birth/growth of the Mississippi Freedom Democratic Party (MFDP); establishing Freedom Schools, community centers, Freedom Libraries, and farming and quilting cooperatives; organizing female domestic workers;

and raising the national consciousness about Mississippi. Bob ended by distributing a list of volunteers with their background information and area assignments.

The bar was opened. Some reviewed the list of volunteer assignments. There was some audible whispering of doubtfulness about suitability.

Jesse Davis looked my way and nodded his concerns. Jesse was short, with bull-frog eyes and crusty in speech. He had been among the original Mississippi Freedom Riders, jailed at Parchman State penitentiary. His mannerisms were jerky. He gave the appearance of a fidgety fugitive in a police lineup.

I decided, unlike him, that I would review the list in the privacy of my room. Experienced SNCC staffers had vetted the volunteers with our input into the interview questionnaire and design of the evaluation grid. So, I thought it best to base my assessment on the orientation outcomes with the volunteers assigned to the Greenville Project.

My attention shifted back to the stage. People were unpacking guitars, banjos, drums, tambourines, and flutes. A songster was now tuning his guitar, plucking the strings, and moaning a familiar Robert Johnson blues:

> "I got to keep movin'
> I got to keep movin'
> Blues fallin' like hail,
> blues fallin' down like hail
> Hmmmm-mmmm, blues fallin' down like hail
> and the dogs keeps worryin' me
> there's a hellhound on my trail
> Hellhound on my trail...."

## Standing in the Need of Prayer, Lord

A journal entry:

"It had become a *laying-my-burdens-down* interlude. Others followed with songs and tales of brutality and heroism. It was all far too familiar. I thought of circumstances where my silence was broken, and my cries went unheard.

I had not, as others had, dwelled in the dungeons where all history is seemingly erased, and the body itself is inscribed with an indecipherable hieroglyphic. I had dodged flying objects, been shot at, spat upon, kicked, and punched. Unlike so many others, I had not been interrogated with the gun pressed against the temple, or endured the bone crunching baseball bat, nor blackjack to the head, nor the flare of the cigarette lighter against genitals. To say nothing of the unsayable sexual indignities suffered by our black sisters in arms.

We had all spent sleepless, periscope-necked nights in cars, or bedded down among the rows of cotton because some rural townspeople were too afraid to provide housing. Many of us had gathered in the dead and dread of moonlit nights, huddled in clandestine backwoods meetings, in black cemeteries wild with brambles and huge nettles everywhere; the diminished tombstones dwarfed by large moss-covered trees, swaying, and rustling a simple ghostly song into the wind. All because some preachers were too scared to open their church doors. These gothic, racialized experiences and memories had brought us to this place, this room, this moment, this catharsis."

I sat listening and surveying the face of each storyteller. I understood that we wore the label marked *fragile—this side up. Handle with care.* I also appreciated the double-entendre of the testimonials. The braggadocious veneer and the subterranean steely resolve of "I got to keep movin'." That "I'se still here." A resiliency best summed up in the Langston Hughes poem "Mother to Son":

> "So boy, don't you turn back.
> Don't you set down on the steps
> Cause you finds it's kinder hard.
> Don't you fall now—
> For I'se still goin', honey,
> I'se still climbin',
> And life for me ain't been no crystal stair."

I knew then, as I had always known—scars and battle fatigue notwithstanding—that we could count on each other. That we were all willing to pay the price of the ticket. "The rain will stop, the night will end, the hurt will fade. Hope is never so lost that it can't be found," wrote Ernest Hemingway.

Cynthia and I left the hall for a late-night campus walk. She shared from her brandy-filled flask. Later she knocked at my door and invited herself in. We drank brandy, chatted, and listened to music.

"We are all fucked," she said.

"Fucked up but not yet fucked," I replied. Laughing. I must have drifted into sleep. Hours later, I heard footsteps and the sound of the closing door. It was love of a different kind.

Later in my room, I reviewed the names and background profiles of the thirteen volunteers assigned to the Greenville Project: six women and seven men. Six were appointed to organize and teach in Freedom Schools, seven to participate in voter registration drives and support the development of the Greenville/Washington County chapter of the Mississippi Freedom Democratic Party (MFDP). All were from highly privileged families and Ivy League schools. All had voiced, in their letters of application, an interest in fighting for equality and justice. A few understood the concepts of institutionalized racism and structural inequalities.

The Greenville SNCC staff totaled ten: two women and eight men. All black. Muriel Tillinghurst was the Project

Director for Washington County and Charlie Cobb shared the responsibility for the Greenville division. We three would coordinate the Greenville Project orientation session. We would devote the next day to arranging the setup of the training room, producing the agenda and handouts, and reviewing audiovisual aids and role-playing scenarios.

The next morning would be an early group breakfast followed by a national press conference with Bob. The campus front lawn was crammed with cameras and microphones. Domestic and international news networks stood restlessly waiting. Bob stood in the glare of flashing lights and the whir of cameras.

"We the People," he began. "I'm going to ask you to think about the preamble to the constitution, and whether you can own it. 'Do ordain and establish,' it says in effect. There is a constitutional class of people who own the constitution. Nowhere in the text does it tell you who the 'we' are. What does it mean to be a constitutional person in this country? Mississippi seceded from the union rather than accept us to be included in 'we the people,' The Mississippi Freedom Summer is about provoking a constitutional crisis to compel Mississippi and the nation to own the constitution.

"But before dealing with the how of what we intend on doing, I would like Fred Anderson to come forward and speak about what it is like to grow up black in Hattiesburg, Mississippi."

"What?" I asked Cynthia. "What did he just say?"

"He invited you to come join him at the podium."

"For what?"

"To speak."

I felt like a hound-treed squirrel. I did a funereal amble to the microphone. I cannot remember what I said. I mumbled the presentation, answered a few questions, and skunked back into the anonymity of my coworkers. It had not been my best moment. The remainder of the press conference was blurred and indistinct.

"You were good, you were on point," Cynthia said.

"I had not planned on doing that," offered Bob.

Had I indeed been good? On point? Good Lord, no.

Busloads of volunteers disembarked in the afternoon. Ruby Doris Smith greeted the volunteers and provided a campus flowchart of assigned dormitories, training rooms, mealtimes, orientation agendas, workbooks, and plenary sessions. The first of which was scheduled for 7 p.m.

Following supper, Bob opened the plenary with his general overview of summer goals, objectives, and activities. He thanked everyone for their participation and courage. He forewarned of the grueling work and dangers ahead. Explaining that our training was designed to reduce risks, mitigate the loss of life, and provide the necessary organizing skills. Dr. Vincent Harding provided a survey history of the state of Mississippi, and chairman John Lewis identified the SNCC workers responsible for their area orientations.

I was first introduced to John Lewis by Sandy Leigh in the winter months of 1964. He had arrived in Hattiesburg for the Freedom Day campaign. He was obviously tired but took the time to speak with me. He was unpretentious and enunciated his words in a meandering Alabama sing-song preacher cadence. Later, we joined others in the voter registration line around the Forrest County Courthouse. It was raining. He smiled at me and said, "Nice day for a demonstration."

He would, thereafter, always greet me with "Homeboys in the house." Never mind that I was from Mississippi, and he from Troy, Alabama. John's strengths lay in his Baptist beginnings and beliefs in goodness, charity, and faith by example—the power of good to triumph over evil. The abiding restorative powers of the beloved community. He was unshakeable in his championing of nonviolence and civil disobedience. No atrocities or ugliness could undermine that faith. It was not naivety, but faith in the evidence of things unseen.

Early the next morning, all trainers gathered in their orientation rooms. We went next door to say hello to Michael Schwerner (CORE organizer), his wife Rita Schwerner, and James Chaney. They introduced us to Andrew Goodman and the other Meridian Mississippi volunteers. Little did I know that this would be the last time that we would see them alive.

The Greenville volunteers filed into the training room. They appeared anxious and tense. Questions erupted across the room.

"It is important that we follow the agenda. The process will answer many of your questions and allay some of your anxieties," explained Muriel. "You really need to digest the history and demographics of Greenville and its surrounding counties. Pay close attention to the history and local dynamics of the Greenville Project. This will not be your regular survey history—the slop fed to you in your college courses. This is foundational stuff. Your life might depend on this."

"I agree with Muriel and Charlie," I stressed. "We know that many of you have questions. We are prepared to provide some answers. But some of your other concerns can only be answered collectively through our actions and interactions. We value discussions. Our approach is to be consensus-seekers. We can debate strategies, but our leadership must be unquestionable. Our interdependence and mutual respect are the linchpins of our safety and for the achievement of our goals."

The white volunteers proved to be eager and rapt learners and became visibly less restrained and more spirited in their communications. There was a noticeable confidence in us as trainers.

## A Storm A'Brewin'

James Chaney, a Black Mississippi Congress of Racial Equality worker, and two Jews from New York—Andrew Goodman, a summer volunteer, and Michael Schwerner, a CORE organizer—departed Oxford, Ohio, on June 21. They had set out to investigate the burning of the Mt. Zion United Methodist Church in Longdale, Mississippi. The church had agreed to serve as a site for the Freedom Library. The three were arrested in Philadelphia, Mississippi—Neshoba County—and released in the middle of the night. This was the official version proffered by Cecil Price, a Neshoba County deputy sheriff and Klan member. They were now considered "missing."

Bob called us together to help us discuss if, how, and what the volunteers should be told. Some were concerned that the news would scare and stampede the volunteers homeward. Most, however, insisted the volunteers had earned the right to know.

What to tell them? Should we just report the facts of the moment? The group had left to investigate a church burning. Had been arrested, released, and were now missing? Eschewing our racial memory, screaming that "missing" in Mississippi meant dead. When to tell them? It was 9:30 p.m. Should we wait until morning? What if overnight word began to spread? A late-night plenary session would be unusual and would ring the fire bells of anxiety.

We decided to knock on doors and summon each to a drill in the auditorium. Bob did not take the stage. He started from the rear of the hall, circulating among the aisles. Leading and encouraging the volunteers in the singing of Nina Simone's *Mississippi Goddam*. Some sang. Most remained quiet. Bob reached the front and locked eyes with the assembly.

"Two of our workers and a volunteer left yesterday to investigate a church burning. Michael Schwerner, James

Chaney, and Andrew Goodman were arrested in Philadelphia, Mississippi. They were released and are now missing. That is all that we know," he calmly detailed. There was a droning wordlessness, silence except for the rustling of chairs. It seemed that none were breathing.

"You had to know. You deserved hearing this from us. This is Mississippi. The question for you to consider is what America is. What is an American? Mississippi is your opportunity to see and experience the fantastical. I promise you that none of you will ever be the same. You will be forced to define what America is to you. What kind of Americans are you? There is danger in that. We need to be wakeful in our approach. Sleepwalking is dangerous and that is why you needed to know. To go or not to go? That is the question. There is no shame in not going. Go now and think about that and discuss it with each other. Call your parents. Tomorrow the media will be all over the campus. Direct all questions to either me or John Lewis. But be clear. There is no guarantee that you will get out of this summer alive. See you at breakfast," he summed up.

It was a long, uncomfortable, and fitful sleep.

We assembled for breakfast. Bob looked over the crowd. "Americans." He beamed. All the volunteers were present and voiced their intention of staying the course. The center had held. There was nothing new to report except that Michael's widow, Rita Schwerner, would be returning to her parents in upstate New York.

The orientation sessions lumbered along, dampened, and heavy, weighed beneath bilious clouds of overhanging fear. National and international media were seized with the disappearance and whereabouts of the three workers. President Lyndon B. Johnson called Mississippi Governor Paul B. Johnson and offered federal assistance. Governor Johnson declined help.

"Those two New York boys are probably sunning on a beach somewhere. They'll show up," he prophesied.

It is instructive that the governor failed to mention James Chaney or speculate on the whereabouts of the young black Mississippian. Meanwhile, President Johnson was feeling the heat. Well-connected and influential white parents were concerned about the potential fate awaiting their sons and daughters in Mississippi. They demanded reassurance. Their unions and corporate affiliations flooded congressional representatives with phone calls, mailings and petitions. Legislators hammered President Johnson. The president called the Mississippi governor again.

"I'm sending you the FBI to assist with getting to the bottom of what happened to those boys, and I mean the black one too," he huffed.

Cynthia and I would soon leave Ohio. Bob and some others would remain to complete the second orientation session. I was growing apprehensive and churlish. I was heavy-handed with the final dos and don'ts with the Greenville volunteers.

"Listen carefully now. Guys at the rear of the room. Please. Tone it down for a moment. Do not drive in integrated cars. No public displays of interracial dating. No driving alone at night. No white volunteers canvassing alone. Always report when leaving the office or Freedom House and declare your destination and returning time. If arrested, do not provide information about local contacts or host families. Any breach of these protocols will result in your being sent home. We need you but will not tolerate risky behavior that might put us all in jeopardy. Especially the local black families that are risking their all by inviting you into their homes," I thundered.

I knew that the shoe was about to drop. I also knew that no orientation could adequately prepare them for the menacing heat of Mississippi daylight, the cloying night

Left to right: Andrew Goodman, James Chaney, and Michael Schwerner. This FBI poster was put up before the bodies were discovered. Knowing Mississippi, the author points out that "the only thing missing are their bodies."

sweats, or the ominous, lurking terrors of delta darkness. The white Mississippi press and public airways were giddy and blood-curdling with threats and plans to repel the northern invasion. The south would rise, yet again, and revenge the ghostly humility of the Lost Cause.

### "Ninety-nine and a half miles won't do."

Cynthia and I departed Ohio for Greenville, Mississippi on June 23. The same day that news broke that the burned and charred station wagon of the three missing workers had been discovered in a thicket of swampy woods near Philadelphia, Mississippi. We sped onwards to Greenville. The volunteers were scheduled to arrive the following morning. I anxiously eyed the speedometer and cautioned Cynthia to slow down.

She pressed the gas, throwing her head upwards, singing and roaring with laughter: "*Satan tries to turn me around, but I don't worry, I don't fret, I've come too far and I'm not tired yet; ninety-nine and a half won't do...*"—Hezekiah Walker, "99 ½"

Arriving in Greenville, Cynthia dropped me at the home of the Turners and set out for her home base in Bolivar County. The Turners were bouncing up and down. Squealing with pleasure at my return. Mr. Turner was, as usual, away on his gospel quartet tour. Mrs. Turner bounced around, placing food on the table. Her two high school daughters informed me that classmates were determined to mount a June 25 downtown protest about the missing civil rights workers.

During mealtime, the droning television screen reported that Mississippi national guardsmen and U.S. Navy divers were dragging the rivers, lakes, and oil-stricken tributaries for the bodies of the three workers. Their draglines ghoulishly hooking and surfacing the waterlogged and bloated torsos of previously unacknowledged and unidentified black victims.

Meanwhile, I felt the urgency to meet and discuss the impending demonstration with the president of Greenville's black Mississippi Student Union. James Blake and his membership were eager and determined to protest.

I met with Mr. Blake in the hallway of Greenville High School. He was a tall, thin boy. Dressed neatly to convey his title. His lips and jaw line contracted, telegraphing the seriousness of his intent and resolve.

"We need your support. But we aim to do this with or without you," he announced.

"We have been ordered not to organize or participate in any demonstrations or other forms of direct action. Voter registration is to be our sole focus," I informed him. I could see the light leave his eyes. "That's likely a final answer. But I will consult with Muriel and Charlie. I will soon get back to you," I said.

Both Muriel and Charlie remained in Oxford, Ohio and were unavailable to take my calls. I left messages but got no reply.

I wanted and felt the need to support these eager and blossoming activists. The clock was ticking. The media continued squawking about the revelation of the burnt-out station wagon and speculating about the fate of the "missing" workers. Fueling the fire and urgency of the students to act. The SNCC office phone was deluged with anxious white parents' requests to speak with their sons and daughters. Dad was pleading for me to return to the safety of Hattiesburg. I reminded him it would be anything but safe for me to be at home.

Mrs. Ella Gaston had called urging me to keep safe. "These white crackers in Hattiesburg and Mississippi are all worked up." The term 'cracker' has its origins in slavery. It describes the overhead, arched whistling snap-crack of the white overseer's whip descending upon black slave bodies.

There were rumors of local whites in unidentified cars and trucks prowling the community and highways. Intent on intercepting the Greenville volunteers. Tensions were high among Greenville black residents. Clouds of fear languished overhead like phantom steam that could not be touched. I reached out to Cynthia in Bolivar County. We arranged for several local black farmers to meet the minivan of volunteers at Benoit, Mississippi and escort them into Greenville.

The volunteers safely arrived in the early morning hours of June 24. They appeared tired and worried. They crowded into the SNCC office and began calling their parents. Two hours later, we completed a tour of the community centers, churches, and black residential areas, and introduced them to their host families. Shortly afterwards, everyone arrived at the Freedom House for lunch provided by local leaders.

## Euphemisms Kill

The Freedom House was, understandably, hissing with talk of the 'missing' workers.

To be black or a civil rights worker and 'missing' is not synonymous in the lexicon of Mississippi.

"Let's stop the obfuscation. James, Andrew, and Michael are dead. The only thing missing are their bodies. As many of you have long suspected," I insisted.

"Our ability to move forward, our safety, our very lives, dictate that we integrate this knowledge into the reality of what it means to breathe and live as black Mississippians," Jesse added.

"All of you will be organizing in the relatively safe environs of Greenville. Only Muriel, Charlie, Jesse, and myself will do the work in the rural enclaves of Washington and surrounding counties," I assured them.

I had intended on alerting them of the impending student protest. But the meeting was interrupted by the appearance of James Blake.

"Have you made a decision about whether you will support our demonstration?" he asked. He had hijacked the process. I was horrified at the notion of allowing black high school students to wade alone into Mississippi's shark infested waters.

I managed to conceal my displeasure. I could read his mind. I was now armed with the benefit of supplemental details. Mrs. Turner had informed me that there were divisions in the student ranks. It seemed that Mr. Blake had run ahead of his support. Some students had been conditional in their support. They were counting on SNCC's buy-in. Some of the parents were supportive of the students but others were dismayed that some of their children were openly defiant of their wishes. I had walked more than a few miles in James Blake's shoes. He was a cat on a hot tin roof, and I was his off ramp. This explained his anxiousness and impatience.

There was a rustling of consternation humming across the room. I pulled James aside and led him to the door.

"You need to trust me to handle this," I whispered.

I returned to the volunteers.

"Mr. Blake represents the Greenville Mississippi black student union. They are upset about the 'missing' workers. His membership, tomorrow afternoon, will be marching in protest at the Greenville Federal Building. They are requesting the support and participation of Greenville SNCC. They are determined to do so with or without our support," I announced.

"But we were told that there would be no demonstrations or direct actions. Only voter registration activities," reminded a volunteer.

"What would Bob Moses think?" asked another.

"Shouldn't we consult with Muriel and Charlie?" another asked.

"I have attempted without success to contact Muriel and Charlie," I replied.

"Shouldn't we apply for a permit to make the protest legal?" Yet another wanted to know.

"What if the permit is refused? Should we protest anyway?"

"This is not our demonstration. We cannot quibble over legalities. We can only set the parameters for our participation," I situated.

I understood their dilemma. The volunteers had been told not to engage in these types of actions. They could be sent packing for disregarding this seminal protocol.

"Our conundrum is whether we can ethically allow the students to go alone. Doing so would erode our credibility in the local black community," I voiced.

Lisa Anderson-Todd, a young white volunteer from Summit, New Jersey agreed that we should support the students. One other volunteer spoke in support. Otherwise, the room remained eerily quiet and restless. And why not? I knew that they would be wading into troubled waters. I also knew that Jesse and I, along with the other SNCC staffers, would have to wade beyond the buoy of Summer Project guidance. God help us should one of the volunteers get injured or arrested.

"What the students require is the support of SNCC. We must and will provide our assistance. Volunteers should adhere to their undertaking not to engage in protest activities," I proclaimed.

I called James and confirmed our support.

"Thank you, Mr. Anderson," he replied.

"It's Fred," I corrected, "and you are welcome."

I placed a call to Clarence Hollingsworth, Sheriff of Washington County. "Fred," he answered, recognizing my voice.

"There will be a demonstration tomorrow afternoon at the Greenville Federal Building," I announced.

"Fuck you," he said, hanging up.

"What did he say?" asked the volunteers.

"He said, 'fuck you,'" I reported.

Charles McLaurin, SNCC Voter Coordinator in neighboring Sunflower County, phoned that he would be coming over with several black high school students to join the protest.

I awoke on the morning of June 25 to see all the white volunteers noisily awaiting departure to the demonstration. I had mistakenly assumed that their compromised position had provided them with a much-desired reprieve. My stomach was revisited by churning anxieties about their defiance, participation, and safety. Oh well. That bell had been rung.

## Baptism

> *"Wade in the water, Children"*
> —Fisk Jubilee Singers, African American jubilee song (1901)

Seventy-five placard-carrying protesters marched on the Greenville Federal Court Building. The action was uneventful, except for a few whites hurling insults. The black students were jubilant with their success—a small incremental rung on the ladder of assertiveness. Jesse and I were relieved that no volunteers had been harmed.

The protest made news in local and state media. White parents sought an explanation as to why volunteers were engaged in protest. A spokesman from the COFO Jackson headquarters issued a press release saying it was not their prerogative to dictate how local black Mississippians should behave. This was a blatant evasion, omitting the participation of SNCC and white volunteers. Bob Moses, who was still in Oxford, Ohio, was besieged by media to explain the Greenville demonstration.

"What demonstration?" he asked. "All participants are aware that the Summer Project revolves around voter registration activities," he concluded.

Stokely Carmichael, SNCC director for the Second Congressional District of Mississippi, arrived in Greenville to meet with Jesse and me. We both knew him and his SNCC bona fides. I instinctively surmised that Stokely had been dispatched by Bob.

Stokely burst through the office door with his usual air of joviality. Smiling, handshaking and back-slapping volunteers.

He announced that he didn't often get the opportunity to visit Greenville. That he was just passing through en route to Jackson. Stopping to say hello to Fred and Jesse. The volunteers glanced warily in my direction. Stokely suggested the three of us go for a walk.

We stopped to purchase three cold Pabst Blue Ribbon beers and sat in the shade of a nearby chinaberry tree. He directly eyed and spoke only to me.

"Fred, we cannot allow ancillary matters"—a term much liked by him—"to distract from our primary goal. Any actions that have the potential to spook white parents and allies will sink our ship. I fully understand the imperative of supporting the black students. But why the participation of white volunteers?" he queried.

"I had not expected and so discouraged their participation," I spoke.

"You and I know that you are a better organizer than that. Well, I am satisfied that you did the best that you could do. Keep up the excellent work," he said.

Back at the office he said his goodbyes. He beckoned me outside.

"You need to manage Jesse. He is a hothead." This was puzzling. But I would soon understand the source of his assessment.

"What the fuck was that?" asked Jesse.

"Just Stokely doing his job," I replied.

### The Pen and the Sword

Greenville volunteer Lisa Anderson-Todd turned out to be a voluminous notetaker and correspondent with her parents. It was her assessment of Jesse Davis that Stokely had referenced.

Her notetaking evidenced a keen perception of the Greenville Project and staff dynamics. She would later write

*For a Voice and the Vote: My Journey with the Mississippi Freedom Democratic Party*. The book is a definitive chronicling of the volunteer experience. She described the players and the contentious debate on the Greenville black student protest and the journey of the Mississippi Freedom Democratic Party. I have only a minor quibble. She sometimes conflated my voice with that of Jesse Davis.

I would last see Lisa on the campus of Tougaloo College. It was the occasion, June 25-29, 2014, of the Mississippi Freedom Summer 50th Anniversary Reunion. She was descending the escalator, heading for an afternoon reunion in Greenville.

"Is that Fred Anderson from the Greenville Project?" she shouted. "Read my book. You are in there," she recommended.

She would, months afterwards, be dead of cancer. Jesse Davis and I would remain friends until his death in 2017. Tracy Sugarman, a journalist, and illustrator also referenced the Greenville Protest in his book, *We Had Sneakers, They Had Guns: The Kids who Fought for Civil Rights in Mississippi*.

We pushed ahead in our efforts to register voters in a parallel strategy of organizing the Mississippi Freedom Democratic Party. We were on course to challenge the seating of the all-white regular Mississippi party delegation at the 1964 National Democratic Convention in Atlantic City, New Jersey.

It seemed, according to author Doris Kearns Goodwin (*Lyndon Johnson and the American Dream*) preordained that Lyndon B. Johnson and Hubert H. Humphrey were to be crowned presidential and vice-presidential nominees. It was known to all that Johnson needed the support of the unreconstructed south to ensure his coronation. It was his 'pined for' opportunity to be elected on his own merits. To escape the dwarfing gleam of Camelot and a slain president.

Meanwhile, the volunteers harnessed their anxieties and remained dogged in their organizing efforts. All of us could see the budding scaffolding of the Mississippi Freedom Democratic Party (MFDP). Black sharecroppers, farmers, and domestics were growing in confidence and political savvy. However, the local black bourgeoisie was restless about being supplanted by 'lower-class' blacks. Many of these upper-echelon blacks served as a pipeline of information to wealthy white families.

One of my prime tasks had been the organizing of a collective of black female domestic workers. These women were employed as help in the homes of white business leaders and political brokers. Including the sheriff and the mayor. They were privy to hushed conversations about white resistance to the power and potential seating of the MFDP delegation. They also funneled information on the identity of black informants. This intelligence enabled us to thwart efforts to insert undesirables into the ranks of the MFDP.

I remember with fondness a meeting at which a black provocateur rose with the intent of derailing the meeting.

The meeting's chairman, a black sharecropper, inquired if the would-be speaker knew Mr. Robert and Mr. Rule.

The man appeared confused. The chairman continued, "Well, they say you are out of order," and swiftly and definitively gaveled the gentleman to his seat.

## Ghosting

> *"A hard rain's a-gonna fall"*
>
> —Bob Dylan (1963)

August 4, 1964: the three 'missing' workers were discovered buried in an earthen dam near Philadelphia, Mississippi. Schwerner and Goodman had been shot in the heart. Chaney had been brutally beaten, shot three times, and castrated.

The discovery dominated the news cycle for weeks, fueling momentum for the MFDP challenge. Lyndon B. Johnson was livid that the unearthing of the bodies had hijacked the national spotlight of the democratic convention and his bid for the presidency. White parents and their allies spearheaded a frontal assault, haranguing their congressional representatives to ensure that their democratic state delegates voted to seat the MFDP.

Our best chances lay with the convention's credentials committee. It was mandated to determine the validity of each state delegation. The MFDP had filed a legal challenge, and the committee was required to hold public hearings. The brief asserted that the MFDP had adhered to all procedures and values of the Democratic Party and should be seated instead of the all-white Mississippi state delegation. The other, lesser avenue was dependent on a convention floor vote, which would require a voice vote by each state delegation.

It was against this backdrop that we made the final preparations to leave Greenville for the convention.

## A Lasting Sense of Grievance

*"Go tell it on the mountain."*

—John Wesley Work, Jr., African American spiritual (1865)

We arrived in Atlantic City on August 23, confident that our allies had engineered a successful lobbying plan. We were both elated and optimistic. The American Civil Liberties Union, NAACP Legal Defense Fund, numerous lawyer guilds, and bar associations had filed Amicus briefs in support of the MFDP challenge. Major labor unions and congressional representatives had pledged support. A seasoned lobbyist was spearheading a public relations campaign and working every state delegation. Religious and secular foundations had granted the funds to support travel and accommodations.

One charity took the lead in transporting the burned and charred station wagon, which we displayed at the convention entrance.

The next morning, the public hearings of the credentials committee would begin. We kept a public demonstration on the boardwalk fronting the convention center: signs and placards in support of the MFDP, along with posters featuring the images of the three slain workers.

Fannie Lou Hamer, the face of the MFDP, would be the first Credentials Committee witness. Every major news network and the eyes of the nation awaited her testimony. She was riveting as she spoke of the brutality and humiliation suffered when she sought to register to vote in Mississippi. The faces of the gathering registered horror and disbelief.

President Johnson, it was reported, watching from the White House, exclaimed to his aide, "That woman will stampede the whole fucking convention." He ordered his aide to issue a release announcing a presidential press conference. Johnson opened the press briefing by acknowledging that there continued to be much speculation about his choice of a vice-presidential running mate. He would soon have something new to announce on that but would take no other questions. He had successfully pre-empted and diverted national attention away from Fannie Lou Hamer's testimony.

Mrs. Hamer and others were crestfallen, but Hamer's testimony, bereft of national media attention, had nevertheless galvanized the support of other convention goers.

President Johnson grew increasingly alarmed about the potential outcome of the committee hearings and feared most a convention floor debate over seating the MFDP. He was in desperate need of a compromise. He pondered whether the all-white delegation and the MFDP would be agreeable to seating two at-large, non-voting MFDP delegates. He would sweeten the bargain with a binding resolution requiring that all future Mississippi state delegations be integrated. He dispatched Hubert Humphrey to do the deal-making.

The all-white Mississippi delegation outright rejected the offer and bolted from the convention in disgust, bathed in the full glare of television lights.

Johnson was disappointed in Humphrey's failure, and made it known that his ascension to the vice-presidential ticket was flapping in the winds of a successful compromise. Johnson also feared that other Southern state delegations might walk in support of Mississippi and doom his prospects of winning the presidency without the assistance of the recalcitrant South. He reached out to Walter Reuther, president of the powerful United Auto Workers Union, inveigling him to garner Martin Luther King Jr.'s support for the compromise. Reuther was an influential donor to King and his Southern Christian Leadership Conference. He commanded King to throw his voice behind the settlement or risk losing their largesse.

### Grifting

> *"These are my principles, and if you don't like them...well, I have others."*
>
> —Groucho Marx (attributed)

Later that evening, Humphrey, haggard and obsequious, couched the compromise as a victory for the MFDP. We were gathered in a large circle with Fannie Lou Hamer in the center. She was seeking advice on the acceptability of the compromise.

She asked Dr. King what he would do. Dr. King spoke eloquently about the achievements of the MFDP and that the bargain validated the long, arduous journey towards full enfranchisement. It was a milestone not to be ignored. Bob hung his head and walked away in disgust. Mrs. Hamer derisively replied to Dr. King, "We didn't come all the way up here for no two seats."

Johnson had prevailed. He had called due every small and sizeable political debt. He had twisted some arms and broken others. The proffered compromise had undermined the hearings and forestalled an unseemly convention floor fight. The South held. The balloons ascended to the rafters; the confetti descended. The party revelers shouted, "All the way with LBJ." Bob was forlorn. We were all dejected. We, along with a motley assortment of black Mississippians and a few white allies, had nearly fomented a political/constitutional crisis but had failed to carry the day.

Bob described the whole debacle as a watershed moment. Until then, the idea had been that you worked within the Democratic Party. However reluctant or tenuous—professed radicalism aside—we were constitutional people. Rooted in the belief that democratic values would triumph over political expediency. America had once again failed to be our guarantor. We were left, in the *I-Have-a-Dream* words of Dr. King, "holding the constitutional promissory note that had come back marked insufficient funds." Atlantic City marked the end of our innocence. It represented the amputation of our earned insurgency. We hobbled and hemorrhaged our way back to Mississippi. But not without having served notice that traditional Democratic Party politics had been found vulnerable. The sins of the reconstruction era, the southern compromise with the unreconstructed South would no longer withstand the resurgence of black populism and newly emerging alliances. We never lost sight, through our truncated tunnel of dispiritedness, that it had been us, unconstitutional people, and the nexus of black enrollment in the American Revolutionary War that helped to secure independence from England and even larger numbers in the American Civil War that ensured democracy's promise. That our resistance to slavery and political steadfastness during the dark purgatory of the Reconstruction Era (1861 to 1900) would not let the nation default on the guarantees of emancipation. A historic juncture in which the United States wrangled with the contentious dilemma of how best to integrate millions of newly freed black Americans into the social, political, and labor systems of the nation. An agonizing interval of southern state sponsored vigilantism unleashed upon newly emancipated slaves. It was the elected blacks, in minority white and majority black state legislatures, that withstood the onslaught, and enacted progressive policies. (See W.E.B. Dubois, *Black Reconstruction in America: An Essay Toward a History of the Part Black Folks Played in the Attempt to Reconstruct Democracy in America, 1860–1880*). It was this tradition of struggle and continuum of resistance which culminated in the Mississippi Freedom Summer and the Mississippi Freedom Democratic Party Convention Challenge (1964) that reshaped the contours of the Democratic Party and motivated President Lyndon B. Johnson to enact the 1964 Civil Rights Act and the 1965 Voting Rights Act. Yet another transformative instance of the activism of blacks, and allies, being the placeholders of democracy. To quote the great black slave abolitionist, author and orator, Frederick Douglass: *"Power concedes nothing without a demand. It never did and it never will...."* Douglass should know as he had worked tirelessly to ensure that emancipation would be one of the outcomes of the Civil War. He recruited black men to fight and two of his sons served in the all black 54th Massachusetts Volunteer Infantry. The history of the Infantry's gallantry was the subject of the 1989 film *Glory* starring Matthew Broderick, Cary Elwes, Morgan Freeman, Andre Braugher, and Denzel Washington. Washington's portrayal of Sergeant Silas Tripp garnered the Academy Awards Oscar for Best Supporting Actor. Douglass's imprint looms large over this quarrelsome and hellacious era of American history. He assumed the roles of Assistant Secretary of the Santo Domingo Commission, legislative council member of the D.C. Territorial Government, board member of Howard University, and President of the Freedman's Bank. He served under five presidents, advisor to President Lincoln, U.S. Marshal for D.C. (1887–1881), Recorder of Deeds for D.C. (1881–1886), and Minister Resident and Counsel General to Haiti (1889–1891). Douglass was also prescient in his understanding of the intersectionality of race and gender. His early recognition and championing of women's agency and full acceptance in the American polity foreshadowed the pivotal leadership roles of black women in SNCC, the Southern Leadership Conference, Congress of Racial Equality, the National Association for the Advancement of Colored People, Students for a Democratic Society, and the feminist movement writ large.

CHAPTER FIVE

# GONE ALREADY

*"Farewell, ole maser, don't think hard of me,
I'm going to Canada. Where all the slaves are free."*

—Harriet Tubman

I had read many of the slave narratives. The Underground Railroad heroism of Harriet Tubman shepherding fugitive slaves north to Canada. Tubman lived nearly a decade in St. Catharines, Ontario. The last stop on the Underground Railroad. Her home base as she ferried slaves northward to Canada. Henry Box Brown escaped to freedom by arranging to have himself mailed in a wooden crate to the free state of Pennsylvania. He lived in England for twenty-five years. He toured and performed as a magician, speaker, and mesmerist until 1889.The last decade of his life (1886–1897) was spent in Toronto, Ontario. He died (June 15, 1897) and was buried in Necropolis Cemetery.

Between two worlds—the suspended horror of flight and the unfamiliar territory of escape. A new cartography of belonging. Little did I know that the internal and public outcomes of the waning Mississippi Freedom Summer and my personal fate would collide with my ancestral struggles and hurl me into the narratives of runaway fugitives seeking exile in Canada. I had not the inkling of an idea of what it meant to be an illegal, living under an assumed identity. How deceptively easy and yet complicated it was to become someone else—nor the ways in which exile influences and transforms perceptions of self. How cyclonic and convulsive a journey is the return to authentic self. "Truth is the property of the national cause," wrote Frantz Fanon. Malleable truth, I would learn, is a hare-triggered snare. The necessity of fabrication was both the process of self-redefinition, narrative cohesion, distancing, and loss of self. Habitual lies are inevitably porous, spawning unnecessary suspicions, unintended betrayals, humiliations, hypervigilance, and self-loathing. Eroding the bonds of trust and reliability along with cascading duplicities that would exact concomitant damage to personal, familial, and marital relationships, as well as children.

These were deceptions that would eventually render doubtful—unbelievable—my disclosures about my true beginnings and journey. Worst of all, I had not anticipated that I could not, for eleven years, reveal my whereabouts or assumed identity, or risk direct contact with my dad, sisters, or grandparents.

Neither did I know that my lies of commission or omission would then and still require penitence and recompense. The denouement of the Mississippi Freedom Summer Project and the road to Albany, Georgia would give rise to the most tumultuous reckoning of all my yesterdays and all my tomorrows.

### Flash Flood

*"Waters Rising, Lord"*

—Jeremiah 47:2

The Mississippi Freedom Summer Project had birthed the Mississippi Freedom Democratic Party (MFDP) and increased the numbers of black voters. The MFDP had galvanized a coalition of Mississippi black and white dispossessed to challenge the core values of the National Democratic Party and the founding tenets of a flawed constitution of the United States of America. "We the people," in the end, meant the white and the powerful.

The project was now slithering to an end. Many white volunteers were leaving for home. Others remained and increased the numbers of the SNCC staff. Many black activists felt that some of the volunteers had been too self-important and autocratic in their interactions with local blacks and were ascending to an inappropriate dominance over the organization. The increased need for armed resistance and growing discontent with some of the new white staff propelled SNCC in the black power direction. Dangers and discord that had been foreshadowed in our heated discussions, in our planning meetings, and the beer summit between Bob and me became evident.

According to Bob, the whole spectrum of race relations compressed, broke down, and would eventually wash us away. SNCC would, despite growing factionalism, continue significant grassroots campaigns in Mississippi, Alabama, Arkansas, and Southwest Georgia. The staff remained divided among those considered "the children of Bob Moses" and the leadership of Stokely Carmichael and others.

I was viewed by many as being a Moses acolyte. This was not entirely inaccurate. It was an uneasy relationship. Many of us continued to believe in SNCC's potential as the organization best suited to push forward the civil rights movement, anti-war initiatives, and collaborations with Latin and African decolonization struggles. The sticking point for us was not about black power. It was more about whether SNCC could remain an organization of organizers. Such a model would continue to require a decentralized and populace-centered decision-making process, as opposed to the proposed highly centralized restructuring that would invest power and decision-making in an executive committee.

## The Albany Movement

*"Young man, your arms too short to box with God..."*

—James Weldon Johnson, *God's Trombones: Seven Negro Sermons in Verse* (1927)

Meanwhile, SNCC was shoring up its operations in Southwest Georgia and shifting its focus to the issues surrounding the dispossession of black farmers.

The Albany Movement (1961–62) had become a storied chapter in the narrative of SNCC organizing. The decision was made to reinvest in the Albany SNCC Project. I was to be transferred to the SNCC office in Albany, Georgia. It was not welcome news. Greenville had become my home away from home. My roots were intertwined with those of the Turner family and my SNCC coworkers. Additionally, my dad, sisters, and grandparents were hopeful that the end of Mississippi Freedom Summer would bring me home to Hattiesburg.

The goodbyes were quick. The next morning, Roy Shields, coordinator of the Southwest Georgia SNCC Albany office, came to pick me up. Roy, a graduate of Franconia College, New Hampshire, immediately informed me that he was always armed and showed me the location of his revolver. We drove straight to the city of Albany, birthplace of "the Genius" Ray Charles and a nightlife that didn't disappoint. But it was not long for my enjoyment. I would be moving on to the small town of Cordele, Georgia. Cordele is the seat of Crisp County known as the "Watermelon Capital of the world." Shipping more than 125 million worldwide. To say nothing of the pecans, peaches, and peanuts. Roy drove and introduced me to Ramona Lockett—the local SNCC contact.

Ramona, twenty-something, was dressed in colors that rainbowed her radiant personality. She was sassy and flirtatious. Her hair was crow's-wing black, springy coils cascading like a dark river down her back. Ramona was always armed. She once used her weapon to scare off white thugs threatening to shoot a white volunteer.

"Fred, you safe with me. These white folks know that I don't mind sending them to heaven. You better get yourself some iron," she warned.

She provided supper and walked me to my assigned quarters. A small, galvanized tin-roofed house with one bedroom, a tiny bathroom, and even tinier kitchen. Ramona appeared in the morning and drove miles to introduce me to black farmers. My assignment was to support black farmers' struggle to stay on the land and maintain ancestral ownership. However, Ramona appeared the next morning and reported that Albany SNCC regional office and SNCC Atlanta were urgently reassigning me to Newton, Georgia-county seat of Baker County— "Bad Baker" in SNCC vernacular. Matters had considerably heated up. Local agriculture board elections were looming, and black farmers were mobilizing, and whites were marauding the black neighborhood and violence was seemingly imminent. She drove me to Newton, Georgia and left me at the home of Irene Jackson.

Rural black activists in the civil rights movement took huge risks, since the whites could withhold loans as a punitive tool. The ability to acquire loans could make the difference between keeping your farm or loss of land. The local white power structure controlled the state and local agencies of the United States Department of Agriculture and used their powers to exclude blacks by secrecy as to agenda, time, date, and location of elections.

I urgently needed to discover the dates, time, and location of upcoming local Agricultural Stabilization and Conservation Services (ASCS) committee elections. Meanwhile, I joined the public education campaign and mobilization of black farmers. It would take weeks of recruitment, training, and familiarity with the voting and electoral process. We had to ensure a sufficient turnout to guarantee the nomination of our slate.

I conscientiously monitored the community notice board at the town square farmers' depot for the announcement of the scheduled nominating meeting. The handwritten notice announced a courthouse meeting on the evening of the next Thursday. We arrived to find the parking lot empty, and the building shrouded in darkness. The week passed without any further notifications. I leaned on my experiences with the Greenville collective of black female domestic workers. I enquired about which black cook was cooking for which white family. Mrs. Jackson knew that the town clerk employed a black cook. She discovered the date, location, and time of the next nominating meeting.

Mrs. Jackson warned that we would be walking into hell. That violence would ensue. That it would be bloody.

### Let Us Prey

*"Feet Don't Fail Me Now"*

—Melvin Van Peebles, *Sweet Sweetback's Baadasssss Song* (1971)

I had successfully recruited forty black farmers. This would ensure enough votes to nominate a slate of black candidates.

Trucks of local whites armed with shotguns, baseball bats, and axe handles surrounded the site. Shouts of "niggers go back!" rained down from the assembled crowd. I shouldered my camera and took up position across the square. I had been instructed to fully document the event.

The black farmers dismounted their trucks, pressed forward, and began to fall like bowling pins. The evening dusk failed to muffle the thudded impact of baseball bats, axe handles, and butts of shotguns to legs, ribs, and heads. My horrified eye was pressed against the lens as my trembling finger clicked the shutter button. The ground was slaughterhouse red.

I shouted, "To the trucks!" and assisted everyone to clamber aboard. The mob gave chase, discharging guns skywards. We took refuge in the Thankful Baptist Church. Neighboring armed black farmers patrolled the perimeters.

This incident, and similar events in Alabama and Arkansas, led the United States Department of Agriculture to conduct a public inquiry. The USDA issued a decree for supervised elections, and five black farmers were elected to the local ASCS committee. It was sad to learn the news that Thankful Baptist Church, the oldest black church in Baker County, established in 1849, was destroyed by fire on December 24, 2018.

Mrs. Jackson drove me back to the Albany SNCC office. An official looking letter awaited: It was a summons to report for induction into the armed forces. I quickly penned a declaration of non-compliance. I filed a field report on Terrell and Baker counties and called to say hello to dad and informed him that I had refused to serve in the army.

"You'll be arrested," he said.

"Not if I can help it," I replied. I stupidly asked him not to worry and said I would keep him informed.

I would be leaving for Atlanta the next day to join Bob and others for the SNCC conference at Gammon Theological Seminary. The conference proved to be a dispiriting experience. Full-blown factionalism was on display. Bob was emotionally drained. It was clear that he and his resolute organizing ideas were no longer welcome in the evolution of SNCC. He had grown uneasy and was sagging under the burden of the messianic adulation associated with his leadership and name. He had never been the type to seek devotees. Bob announced that he was dropping his surname and would only use his middle name, Paris, and would take a leave of absence from SNCC.

He returned to New York. I returned to Albany, Georgia.

### Which Way, Lord

Weeks later, I received an invitation to join Bob, Herman Carter, and seven other SNCC Mississippi workers in New Orleans.

Herman, too, had already refused induction into the army. He was originally from Hampton, Virginia and was a beanpole of a figure: tall, lean, with angular features, crowned with a salt and pepper Zapata mustache. He had exceedingly long, tapered fingers that were in constant motion, carving the air, orchestrating his softly spoken words.

The all-black New Orleans meeting, dubbed the "Roots Conference," focused on energizing decolonization alliances, exploring and defining our role in the newly emerging black consciousness movement (BCM), and a dialogic relationship with allies. We drafted and distributed a working proposal. Bob submitted his resignation as director of Mississippi COFO and SNCC Mississippi field operations.

We convened another two-week retreat in Alabama in July 1966 to think through and finalize our statement of purpose. Unforeseen circumstances upended our plans: Bob received a draft board notification to report for induction. He, of course, declined the offer.

Herman and I accompanied Bob to New York, where two former women SNCC workers had arranged jobs for us at a nursery school. The nursery school jobs became a cover while we worked in the shadows getting ready to flee the country.

Because the draft board was already trailing the two of us, Bob, fluent in French, traveled to Montreal, Canada and rented a place in the Little Burgundy district. The epicenter of Montreal's English-speaking black community.

Herman and I would depart for Canada in two days' time. Bob would join us in several weeks.

### Dreaming Freedom

> *"You have navigated with raging soul*
> *Far from the paternal home,*
> *Passing beyond the sea's double rocks.*
> *And now you inhabit a foreign land."*
>
> —Euripides, *Medea*

Wakeful rehearsal of our new identities; two sleepless, distressful nights of flighty possibilities of being seized at the border. We would, entry denied, be handed over to American customs agents and eventually jailed for draft evasion.

Edgy, early morning boarding of the Trailways bus, each of us bearing two soon-to-be-discarded U.S. social security cards. A shape-shifting bye-bye to America. Herman seated up front and me in the rear. A strategy designed to ensure that both, or at least one of us would cross over.

The bus was mostly occupied by McGill University students returning from a New York City weekend of frivolity. Their exploits expressed in an effortless segue between the English and French languages. The bus hugged the lines and kissed the curves through the rolling hills and small towns of upstate New York. One of the students asked if I was going to Montreal.

"Yes, for a weekend visit," I replied.

"Your first visit to Canada?"

Yes, I said.

"Read this," he said, handing me a book entitled *The Loved and the Lost*.

It was the story of a young, restless uptown white girl's misunderstood entanglements with black musicians in the jazz clubs "below the hills" in 1950s Montreal. The book provided a smarmy glimpse into some of the racial interactions and attitudes of the day. The "below the hills" jazz clubs were in the black neighborhood that would soon become our initial home ground.

Passengers were twitching. The bus down clutched to a slow crawl. I closed the pages on the young white girl's coming of age saga. Ahead was a greystone building. A wind-blown red emblazoned maple leaf flag crowned the building. The driver cranked the door open. A cold November wind whistled down the aisle. A bearded, clipboard-bearing agent boarded, cheerfully greeted the driver, surveyed the passengers, and approached Herman. I imagined reading the cartoon bubble script floating above Herman's head: *It's now, sink or swim*.

"French or English?"

"Citizenship?"

"Destination?"

"Business or pleasure?"

"How long do you plan on staying?"

There was no request for proof of identity! I was relieved but still tense. The agent now stood in front of me.

"English or French, sir?"

"Citizenship?"

"Can I see some ID, sir?"

He had not asked this of Herman! I produced my U.S. social security card.

"Nothing with a picture?"

"No, sir. I don't drive and I do not have a passport," I said. This is not looking good, I thought. I imagined the familiar clanking of the jailhouse door. Had I misread the balloons above Herman's head?

"Destination?"

"Business or pleasure?"

"A weekend visit with friends at McGill University," I replied.

"Where will you be staying?"

"With friends on St. Antoine Street," I answered.

"Welcome to Canada."

"Thank you," was my rehearsed answer. But my blubbered tongue was flat, heavy, and unresponsive. I sat like a flailing, oxygen-deficient, beached beluga whale.

The driver closed the door and sped towards Montreal—America receding in the rear-view mirror. There was much that I would miss. But my feelings were not unlike those of Mississippi author Richard Wright on leaving his country for France: "I was not sorry when my ship sailed past the Statue of Liberty."

This much I knew. Black men and women would no longer dwell in the shadow of cruelty and the falsity of a white manhood, which still seeks lost confederate dreams; blasted hopes long buried in civil war graveyards; clearance sales of white sheets that are no longer capable of striking fear in even the smallest of black girls and boys. No. The South would not rise again. The ashes of that empire had long ridden the winds and floated out to sea. The secret was out. The South is our home as much as theirs.

The bus plowed onward. The black ribbon of the road sheathed with squalling snow. Heat prickled across my skin and tremors seized my hands, arms, and legs. Tears trickled down my cheeks. I could barely discern the snow-covered landscape banked with scraggy, barren trees, and the headless buildings dwarfed by the fleecy skyline. My fogged vision conjured a diminutive black figure trudging through the whiteness, and her celebratory voice calling out to me: "And I never run my train off the track, and I never lost a single passenger." It was an apparition of Harriet Tubman, the Moses of her people.

Herman joined me at the rear of the bus, gently squeezing my knee. Grinningly winking his left eye.

CHAPTER SIX

# SWING LOW, SWEET CHARIOT

*"A city that is set on a hill cannot be hidden"*
—Matthew 5:14

Towering on the horizon was a steel Lego-like truss, spanning the green-blue waters of the St. Lawrence River. The Trailways bus strained uphill, crossed the Jacques Cartier Bridge, and descended through a spectacle of snow-blanketed oil tankers, industrial towers, soot-spewing smokestacks, and veered onto Dorchester (now René-Lévesque) at Peel and wheeled into the bus terminus.

We walked to Dunn's Café. The interior was decked out in holiday tinsel and Bing Crosby crooned a honeyed version of "White Christmas." We had a coffee and studied Bob's handwritten directions to Guy and St. Antoine Street. *Walk west on Dorchester, don't go past the Northern Electric building, turn left on Guy, proceed to St. Antoine.* It was a longer than anticipated journey. The snow was high and swirling. Guy to St. Antoine Street was a downhill walk. The wind was brisk and penetrating. Our address was directly across from the Salvation Army Men's Hostel. Indigent residents were bundled against the cold, smoking cigarettes, swigging beer, and downing open canisters of whiskey.

Our lodging was a red brick structure of eleven dwellings, situated in an open courtyard with a wooden snow-laden balcony belted by an abandoned plot at the west of the building and a greasy spoon burger, hotdog, and french fry canteen to the east.

The door lock resisted the key but reluctantly surrendered with a squeaky opening into darkness and iciness. Herman flipped the light switch and cockroaches scurried across the floor and into wall cornices. Ceiling lights revealed a tiny bathroom, sink, toilet, and shower festooned with a corroded shower head and faucets. The kitchen featured a Hotpoint gas range with four elements, oval oven, low-level Westinghouse fridge, three overhead cabinets, drawers, and a small collapsible table. There was an assortment of grimy plates, cups, pots, and cutlery. There were small windows in the bathroom, kitchen, bedroom, and a large sitting room window overlooking the balcony. The condition of the weather-worn wooden posts and railing did not inspire confidence. Off the hallway was a small sitting room with a rumpled couch, four small, stained armchairs, a closet, and a large bedroom equipped with three army cots.

I twisted the valves on the white wall-mounted radiators. The pipes hissed, gurgled with water, and hiccupped into action. We opened all the taps until the water ran clear and dined on canned sardines with saltine crackers. Herman eyed our surroundings and sighed. We exchanged joyless glances and agreed that tomorrow would be devoted to house cleansing.

"Beats sleeping in cars and cotton fields," I said.

We shared a much-needed moment of weightlessness. The heat was sluggish in its response to the babbling radiators. I climbed into my cot fully dressed and hunkered beneath the surplus army store blanket.

## Harlem of the North

We awoke to a nippy bedroom and apartment. We downed coffee and toast at the downstairs greasy spoon and chatted about immediate needs.

We had enough funds to cover six months of rent and other living necessities. We reasoned that the urgency was to select our assumed identities and speculated on how to secure forged documents that would provide cover for our illegal status, gain employment, enrolment in university, and, if need be, emergency travel.

We stepped out and looked up and down the narrow east-west expanse of St. Antoine Street. The denizens of the Salvation Army, backs to the wind, lined the concrete façade like crows on a wire. Stamping their feet against frost and smoking stubs of reclaimed cigarette butts.

We ambled westward through narrow streets squeezed between long rows of grey dwellings. The sun illuminated a gabled church bell tower. Its glistening spire blessed by the christening of falling snow. We traveled south on Atwater Avenue. Union United Church stood at the corner of Atwater and Delisle street—Montreal's oldest black Church. We read the founding plaque, which announced that it was founded in 1907 as a place of worship for blacks denied entry into all-white churches.

Across the square, people jostled among the stalls of the Atwater Market. The air was scented with wood shavings, pine needles, and the balsamic aroma of freshly cut Christmas tree. A black lady and her little boy struggled under the weight of their purchased tree. We offered to help. She said that they lived near the NCC—Negro Community Centre.

The Centre was located east of the Atwater Market on Coursol at Canning Street. It was a four-story grey stone building founded

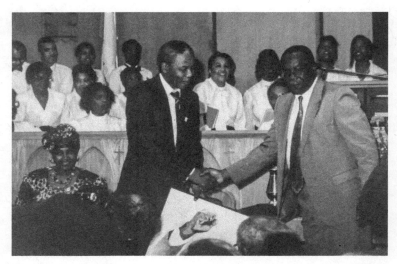

Nelson Mandela and Fred Anderson at the Union United Church, Montreal, Quebec, June 20, 1990, Montreal's oldest black congregation. I was proud as executive director of The Society for the Promotion of Quebec Black Artists to present to Mandela an original portrait by one of our member artists. (Photo courtesy of Andrew Cummings)

in 1927 under the leadership of Reverend Charles H. Este and the worshippers of Union United Church. It was evident that the building was originally a church. The front façade featured a rose window over a deep arched entrance and to the right was a bell tower rising above the building's pitched roofs. The Centre served as the cultural and recreational hub of Little Burgundy's black residents. Providing activities ranging from dance, piano instruction, day camps, daycare, basketball gymnasium, social clubs, auditorium, banquet halls, kitchen, citizenship classes, dental services, employment service, counselling, credit union, and a library devoted to black history and literature.

We entered the front lobby, flanked leftward by a glass-paneled reception office and, to the right, downward steps to a lower level. We were greeted and ushered into the office of the secretary. Her office gave entry to the lower-level spacious quarters of Executive Director Mr. Stanley Clyke.

He provided us with a tour of the Centre. Throughout, we witnessed black participants of all ages mirthfully engaged in activities. It was not just recreation but cultural engagement. We met a diverse sampling of the black diaspora from Nova Scotia and the Caribbean, expatriate black Americans, Africans, Haitians and native-born black Canadians. We were captivated by our dissimilarities but reassured by the evidence of common roots and aspirations.

It had been a wondrous and fatiguing day. We stopped by a hardware store, purchased a shovel, cleaning products, cockroach powder, and headed home. I shoveled and heaved snow over the balcony, breathing a sigh of reprieve when the wood planked flooring did not collapse. We drank ginger beer and ate beef patties. Both were fiery and delicious. We cleaned and sanitized the apartment into the early morning hours. Tomorrow we planned to explore the east of St. Antoine and intersecting thoroughfares. The radiators were warm to the touch. Sleep crawled and eased in on Herman's soothing snoring.

In the early morning, the wind began to howl. Snow and sleet pelted the windows. I raised the small collapsible kitchen table. We cupped, blew into our hands, and huddled over mugs of instant coffee.

Later, hands in pockets, shoulders hunched and leaning into the wind, we set out eastward along St. Antoine Street. This stretch of the street still featured some of the iconic bars, clubs, and eateries that had earned Little Burgundy the designation "Harlem of the North." The Welcome Hall Mission, opened nightly at 8:30 p.m., served unshaven and poorly clad men a plate of free stew and a bed for the night. Saint Anthony Padua Church was on the south side and Whitey's Hideaway Cocktail Lounge, boasting the finest in southern cuisine, was tucked into Aqueduct Street. The Canadian Royal Legion Post #50 was at the corner of Lusignan; a favorite watering hole for black WWII veterans—I later read a vitriolic and demeaning account penned by the son of the owners of the Legion building. The book proved to be illustrative of the racial animus and stereotypes of the period. The Black Bottom Jazz Club was open 10 p.m. to 10 a.m. on Thursday, Friday, and Saturday. It specialized in chicken wings, Southern soul food, and some of the best modern-day jazz. There were barbershops and pool halls. The acclaimed Rockhead's Paradise was on the south side of St. Antoine.

Rockhead's, the three-story show bar, had been home to the likes of Duke Ellington, Cab Calloway, Ella Fitzgerald, Billie Holiday, Nina Simone, Fats Waller, Dizzy Gillespie, and Sammy Davis.

The Harlem Paradise Club rivaled Rockhead's as the best club for Black entertainment. A window banner proclaimed: "All Here at the House of Live Action—Alive and in Living Colour."

Blacks from the West Indies, Nova Scotia, and the United States migrated to Little Burgundy because it was a railway hub. They worked the trains as sleeping car porters and railway hands. The women worked as domestics in the homes of wealthy whites in Westmount, Town of Mount Royal, and Outremont. It was a hard life characterized by low wages and racial discrimination.

The city people on the hill were contemptuous of Little Burgundy— "the debaucherous jazz scene and low-life social scene," the poverty, and the increasing numbers of newcomers. The city below the hill was, already in 1966, slated for the wrecking ball. Designed and decreed for urban renewal, but not without a fight. A coalition of black community, anti-poverty, and religious groups fought valiantly to save the district. However, Little Burgundy would soon be demolished, and all the black-owned businesses, institutions, and residences expropriated by the city of Montreal. Gone to ashes. Dispersed to Lasalle, Cote des Neiges, and other neighborhoods.

We turned south on Guy Street to Notre Dame and made some purchases at the Salvation Army store—a cast-iron skillet, coffee pot, small AM/FM radio, small screen black and white television, winter boots, scarves, gloves, toques, and long winter coats. We were now equipped like Matthew Henson, blackfootin' through the snows of the North Pole.

I had also selected two hardcovers from the book bin. An English translation of Gabrielle Roy's *The Tin Flute: A Bitter-Sweet Love Story*. The novel unfolds in the Saint-Henri-Petite-Bourgogne-Saint-Charles districts, our home ground. A French-Canadian, Irish, and black working-class neighborhood. The second book was *Two Solitudes*, a novel about the perceived lack of communication between English-speaking and French-speaking Canadians.

We hailed a taxi to Steinberg's grocery store and stocked up on meats, vegetables, a few bottles of wine, and taxied home. I prepared our first home-cooked meal: creole chicken wings, rice, gravy, and fried okra. We reveled in the aromas, tastes, and longings for home. Later we smoked Canadian cigarettes—Export A brand—drank wine and listened to jazz on our new radio.

"Call me Bill." Herman announced.

"What?" I asked.

"My new name, Bill Williamson," he explained.

"Hello Bill," I greeted. "Call me Clifford, Clifford Gaston," I parried. It was the name of my nearest childhood friend and schoolmate.

It was not, in retrospect, a wise selection. The intended goal was not to provide the hounds with any trail of familiar scents.

We clinked our glasses, drained the dregs, and went to bed.

The next morning—Bill still snoring—I walked across the street to the public phone booth and deposited some coins and dialed the number associated with Bob Moses.

"Hello, the apartment is fine," I said. Our code for 'package delivered safe' and hung up the receiver.

I next placed a call to Hattiesburg neighbor Ella, Clifford's mother. She would be my sole eleven-year conduit for messages to dad and family.

"Son, it's good to hear your voice," her muffled voice intoned.

"I am living across the river," I reported.

"Don't drown, be a strong swimmer," she encouraged. "Francis is no longer with us," she reported and hung up. We would become dueling jazz musicians, improvising but always returning to a common treble-clef-coded rhythm.

She was a community mother, and all trusted her with their children. She had been a childhood confidante and mentor. I knew that I could trust Mrs. Ella because her personal story of activism and drama of evading arrest had schooled her in the arts of subterfuge.

I recrossed the street and entered the downstairs grease emporium. My stomach was recoiling from the news of Francis's, my grandmother's, death. The unctuous fumes of recycled grease further heaved my emotional imbalance. I was impervious to the wetness trickling down my cheeks until the salty tears met my tongue. I was startled by the waitress serving a cup of steaming coffee until she gently caressed my shoulder. My relationship with my grandmother had frayed due to her relentless needling and recriminations against dad for not preventing me from leaving home. It had been a long time since I had seen her. She had on my last home visit, made her special rice pudding. I have spoken of her green thumb and how she groomed the soil with chicken manure, and how her front yard had become redolent with the luscious fragrances and peacock-colors of a bounty of lilacs, daisies, roses, sunflowers, black-eyed Suzie's, lilies, daffodils, marigolds, gardenia, hydrangea, coronations, tulips, and forget-me-nots. How every visitor, stranger or not, always left with a small twine-tied bouquet of forget-me-nots.

Oh, how I shall miss the childhood backyard memories of her roiling cauldron of a black pot at hog-killing time and the alchemy of her homegrown cures. The sugary taste of her jams and preserves. The magic light that shone on her shelf-lined, green-tinted bottles. I will miss the quilting bees that allowed a young boy's entry into the circle of swirling tall tales and the cherished repository of pain and resiliency of Hattiesburg blacks. But most of all, I will miss how she wordlessly wrapped me in love and surety following the death of her daughter, my mother. She was a woman of few words but her touch, her smile, a nod of her bandana wrapped head, a tap of her walking cane and the invitation into her kitchen, never failed to convey self-regard and love. Nothing could match the gifting of one of her hand-stitched quilts. How I wish that I had one of her heavy embroidered tapestries strung over my upstairs cot, shielding me against the irascibility of the winds, snows, and ice of the Canadian winter.

Grandmother, I wish you warmth and a coffin laden with front yard flowers. I went upstairs to advise Bill. He was sipping his coffee and could see that I was distressed. I informed him that I had made the coded call to Ella Gaston and got news of my grandmother's death.

"Damn," he said, and stroked my head. "You can't go," he cautioned.

I knew.

"Let's go," he said, and we walked the five blocks to Canadian Legion Post #50 on Lusignan Street. There was a sparse crowd of black veterans. We munched salted peanuts and quenched our thirst with cold bottles of Labatt 50 beers. Obvious eyeballing confirmed that we were newbies.

"Where you boys from?" asked a veteran.

"From the States," we replied.

"Well welcome, my name is Jimmy," he boomed. "I lived in Chicago for a spell, but I missed Canada. I am originally from Halifax, Nova Scotia, the black settlement of Africville. Ever heard of that? I guess not," he slurred.

Jimmy explained that Africville was a Nova Scotian settlement established by black Nova Scotians of different origins. Many were descendants of formerly enslaved African Americans from the original American colonies. They had been black Loyalists during the American War of Independence and the War of 1812. "But all that will soon be demolished. Urban renewal they call it," he said, tossing some commemorative beer drops over his left shoulder.

"Your friend doesn't speak much," he said to Bill.

"He just got news of his grandmother's death," replied Bill.

"Oh, that ain't good. Guess you going home soon," he said. The table was silent.

"Hope I didn't say anything wrong," he inquired, waving the waiter over with more pints of beer and saluting the departing server.

"You boys aren't draft dodgers. Are you?" he asked. "There are lots of them in Montreal. But you the first two black ones that I know of. Well, I served Her Majesty in WWII, and I say each to his own. I don't hold nothing against you. We black, ain't we," he reckoned. "Well, I'm here every Thursday night," he told us, as he wobbly clambered to his feet, saluted, shoved his chair under the table and was gone.

We downed our beers, stood, and attempted a teetering salute to the remaining veterans and lurched homewards, pissing in the snow, and sputtering freedom songs into the raw winds.

Sleep was a booze-fueled magic carpet ride. The cot teeter tottered above the clouds hovering over Hattiesburg, tilted and catapulted my limp body into the ethers. I was in free fall, screaming and horrified until I realized that I could fly. I was cruising over Mount Bethel Baptist Church. I could see the hearse—the pallbearers measured stride and the white-gloved hands of the black-suited attendant, closing the entrance doors.

"Wait for me!" I moaned. I furiously thrashed and retracted my wings in hopes of parachuting downwards, but the warm winds hoisted me ever higher. I was breathlessly wailing, "No, let me down, open the door."

"Life's a voyage that's homeward bound," prophesied Herman Melville.

"Wake up, it's okay, all is good." It was shoulder-shaking Bill. He gently dabbed my face with a cold washcloth and handed me a cigarette and a cup of coffee.

I called Ella Gaston for news of the funeral.

"Hello," she answered. "Full church and a garden of memories. It was a sunny bright day except for some expected buzzards."

'Buzzards' was our code word for FBI agents on the scene.

### Paris of North America

We climbed the hill up Guy to Ste. Catherine, passing Shinehart's clothing store, Redfeather Social Services, and the Montreal Children's Hospital. The Forum, home of the peerless Montreal Canadiens hockey team, dominated the skyline. The Toe Blake-owned tavern was across from the Forum. Blake was coach of the seven-time winning Stanley Cup Champion team.

His tavern, like most others, was a male fortress. Quebec taverns were the preferred venue for male camaraderie, peanuts, saltine crackers, cheese blocks, pickled eggs, pig knuckles, and watching televised hockey games. I can remember mothers, anxious that dads would drink up the milk and bread money, sending young male children to tavern doors with orders to wave and finger dad in the direction home. Quebec legislated against men-only taverns in 1979. Ste. Catherine Street is the downtown mainstay of business, entertainment, go-go window dancing, peep shows, sex cabarets, and stately churches. Mark Twain remarked on his 1881 visit to Montreal, "This is the first time I was ever in a city where you couldn't throw a brick without breaking a church window."

We stopped to admire the venerable architecture of St. James United Church and Christ Church Cathedral. Twain could have said the same of the theatres on every corner—famous for their live shows and movie reels. There was the York on the southwest corner of Ste. Catherine and Mackay, Capitol, Palace, Imperial on Bleury, Loew's on Ste. Catherine just west of Mansfield. Nat King Cole, Tony Bennett, and Harry Belafonte performed at the Seville on Ste. Catherine at Chomedey and the Strand, corners of Ste. Catherine and Mansfield. The Esquire Show Bar was on Stanley Street just south of Ste. Catherine. This rhythm and blues nightclub had been home to Chubby Checker, Bo Diddley, Fats Domino, Tina Turner, Ray Charles, and Little Richard. There was also the Venus de Milo Room at Ste. Catherine and Dorchester Square.

Amidst all of this we found a door further up Stanley Street, emblazoned with stenciled lettering advertising the office of the War Resisters' League of Montreal.

There were also reminders of our inescapable history. We saw souvenir shops openly displaying confederate flags, decals, and other memorabilia of the lost cause. There were denigrating figurines of black lawn jockeys, watermelon eating "darkies," and Aunt Jemima spoons and kitchen jars.

We continued past Simpson's and Morgan's department stores. Here we stopped to read a plaque dedicated to Jefferson Davis, president of the southern confederacy. Davis, after the surrender of the confederate forces, had been charged and jailed for treason and fled to Montreal in 1867. He was housed in the home of John Lovell, the then-site of the Morgan's department store. The United Daughters of the Confederacy had commissioned the plaque in his honor in 1957. It was, after much protest, removed in 2017. "History does not repeat itself," according to Mark Twain, "but it often rhymes."

We walked up Metcalfe to De Maisonneuve and entered Bens Deli. The three-story brown-brick building was worshiped for its smoked meat and club sandwiches. Lunch-time regulars lined up around the block. It was a long wait. We finally approached the stainless-steel edged counter, sat on the chrome stools, and ordered the smoked meat and fries with strawberry milkshakes. The walls were covered with photographs of media personalities, politicians, writers, world class entertainers, and athletes who had occupied a booth or these same stools. Everybody that day was making a fuss over Mordecai Richler and Roch Carrier. All of which meant nothing to us. I would later meet, interact with, and witness their famous literary careers. The smoked meat sandwich did not disappoint.

We continued down Sherbrooke past the Roddick Gates of McGill University, turned onto McTavish, and ascended the steep wood stairway to the lookout atop Mount Royal. A nearby tour guide was explaining the sights to his charges. The wind was blustery above the city, but the sun was high and provided a bright view of the harbor, St. Lawrence River, and the outstretched wings of the Virgin Mary aloft Notre-Dame-de-Bon-Secours Chapel in Montreal's old port, known as the sailor's church. We visited the mountain-top chalet for warmth and bowls of steaming, frothy hot chocolate. Below, children twirled, skating the frozen lucent surface of Beaver Lake. The crackle of the ice and their yells resounded through the snow-capped maple and pine trees.

It was a weary descent and leg-tingling walk back to St. Antoine. We had gained some appreciation of the span and diversity of Montreal.

A black man, woman, and two small children entered the apartment across the hallway. New tenants? No, they had been away visiting a sick relative in Truro, Nova Scotia. Their children were named Tiffany and Walter. The woman, Eugenie, worked as a domestic and Sylvester Williams was employed as a rail hand in the Canadian Pacific Railway yard. We exchanged our counterfeit vitals and welcomed them back to Montreal. Later, Sylvester knocked on our door and invited us to supper.

Their apartment was larger and more tastefully furnished than ours. Their children were bouncy, curious, and well behaved. We dined on creamy, fluffy mashed potatoes, green beans, crispy fried oysters, and curried rice, and drank dark rum and talked of black life in Nova Scotia, Montreal, and Mississippi. I extended an open invitation to supper, and we said our goodbyes.

The next day we would visit the office of the War Resisters' League.

## CHAPTER SEVEN
# MARINERS ALL

> *"Call me Ishmael"*
> —Herman Melville, *Moby Dick* (1851)

> *"A leopard is chasing me, and you are asking me if it's a male or female?"*
> —African Proverb

The War Resisters' League was a small walk-up in congested quarters. A crumpled sofa, littered desk, filing cabinet, begrimed telephone, typewriter, bulletin board, maps of Montreal and the province of Quebec, a bookshelf laden with dusty-yellowed pamphlets and anti-war reading, and a dehydrated potted African violet on the windowsill.

James Miller was the office manager. He explained the many supports available to draft dodgers. He was very pointed in his questioning and apologized by explaining that the colony of Montreal exiles was riddled with imposters and informers. We informed him that we were surveying the market for official identity documents.

"Be careful, there are a lot of scam artists in the market," he warned, adding, "I have a secure contact that can get you anything you need but it will cost you."

"How do we contact him?" I asked.

"You don't," he replied. "You deal through me," he emphasized.

"How much?" I asked.

"Five-hundred dollars and that's a bargain for good work," he offered.

"How long will it take?" I asked.

"Well, first I have to do as much as humanly possible to verify your authenticity. I have some friends State-side that worked in the civil rights movement. I will make some calls tonight and tie up your story. Come back and see me tomorrow morning. Come prepared with written particulars for your Canadian birth certificate and social insurance card."

I placed a phone booth call to our New York contact. I explained the circumstances of the document search and asked if Bob Moses had settled on a new name.

"Yes, Herb Robinson," she reported. "Are you sure about this contact?" she asked.

"It's a gamble worth the taking," I assured her.

We were mid-morning back at the War Resisters' office.

"Your story checked out," reported James Miller. "You got the written details?" he asked. "You got the money?"

I handed it over.

"Okay, don't come back here. Meet me for coffee in four days at Murray's restaurant on Ste. Catherine at Guy."

Bill and I sat nervously in a window booth. James Miller was late. Had we been scammed, we wondered. He entered and extracted a legal-size manilla envelope from his knapsack and slid it across the checkered tablecloth. My twitchy fingers unsheathed the papers. A crisp replica of a Canadian birth certificate replete with Truro, Nova Scotia as place of birth, and names, parent names, midwife names, embossed with the provincial seal of Nova Scotia.

Miller explained that the midwifery touch was added because hospital birth records were too easily searched. The accompanying document was a laminated card replica of a Service Canada-issued Social Insurance Card, complete with a mirror image of the government maple leaf decal. It was well-spent money.

"I don't want to see you guys again," warned Miller.

I carefully returned the documents to the envelope and bid him farewell. Bill and I were euphoric. We were now legal illegals.

Nearing home, we stopped in the Lusignan Street Canadian Legion Post #50 and celebrated with peanuts and beers. I lifted the receiver of the pay phone, deposited coins, and dialed the New York number.

"Signed, sealed, and delivered," I reported and hung up.

We picked up an extra-large all-dressed pizza and beers. Our neighbor Sylvester knocked on the door. The wife and kids were out at the Negro Community Centre. He joined us in eating pizza and downing beer.

"Are you guys truly draft dodgers?" he asked.

We looked perplexed.

"Oh, I know Jimmy. The veteran you spoke with at the Legion lodge. He means well but doesn't keep anything to himself. He will sell you the shirt off his back. That is if you are willing to pay above market price. Are you guys legal?" he asked.

"We are good," we answered.

"I know some black seamen in Nova Scotia. They can get their hands on anything. Let me know if you should need anything, and I mean anything. We are neighbors, eh?"

We clinked our beer bottles—neighbors.

"Just remember that you can't trust everybody. There are people in Little Burgundy that are desperate for a break, a second chance, a weed high. They will sell their mother, newborn, or trade information for a quick fix or dismissed charges. Black exception notwithstanding, you hear what I'm saying?"

The Halifax and Truro reminisces of Jimmy and Sylvester, unbeknownst to them, had provided the blood and sinews—the skinning—of our new Nova Scotian identities. The two of them also enlightened us about the history of slavery in Canada, the current climate of racial hostilities, and discrimination in Montreal.

The wet morning snow was weighty, and the wind was hulking up Guy Street. I entered the Bell Canada building to request installation of a residential telephone line.

"Your name, sir?" asked the attendant.

"Clifford Gaston," I replied. I provided the requested address and apartment number.

"Identification, driver license, or social insurance card will do."

I produced the glossy, officially embossed card.

"Thanks, sir. We can install your line tomorrow morning between 9 a.m. and 12 noon. Will there be somebody home? This is your new telephone number."

"Yes, I will be home," I confirmed.

"Welcome to Bell Canada, sir," he said, closing the deal.

I walked back down the hill, oblivious to the snow and wind. I felt toasty cloaked in the warmth of my Scotian beginnings. Bill flashed a smile of acknowledgement and relief that I had not been detained. We passed the day reading, listening to music, and talking of home. Jimmy Witherspoon backgrounding our lonesomeness, crooning, "Tell Me How Long This Train Been Gone."

Later we walked up St. Antoine to attend the late-night opening of the Black Bottom Jazz Club. Thelonious Monk, improvisational jazz pianist, father of modern jazz and bebop style, was the guest artist. The tiny venue was packed, and Monk and his quartet sweated masterfully through two sets. Applause and shouts of amen rippled the club. We ate chicken wings, ribs, and drank cups of black coffee sometimes spiked with under-the-table whiskey courtesy of nearby patrons. I used the club pay phone to contact New York and report our new telephone number and next day installation. We and other bleary-eyed patrons crawled out at the 10 a.m. closing hour.

Bill went to bed. I curled up in an armchair, nodding one eye open and listening for the door knock of the Bell Canada man. He arrived near noon and busied himself snipping and stapling a cable along the baseboard, inserted the phone jack, plugged it into a wall outlet, and placed the black unit on our water-stained wooden telephone stool and said, "All set." It would be good to no longer have to brave the cold to make use of public phone booths. However, I would not use our residential phone to contact Ella Gaston.

I pulled the leftover chicken from the fridge; washed, peeled, and cubed potatoes; sliced and diced assorted vegetables; added water; seasoned with a bouquet of spices; and kneaded a dough mixture for dumplings. I placed the pot on the stove to simmer and went to bed. Later, we slurped our chicken and dumpling soup and sopped the juices with hunks of French baguette. Bill suggested a late-night walk along the oldest street in Montreal. Notre-Dame Street is an avenue of antique shops and the site of the Palais de Justice, Château Ramezay, the resplendent architecture of Notre-Dame Basilica, and Hotel de Ville de Montreal (the City Hall). The lampposts and overhead wires were illuminated with flashing Christmas lights and holiday bunting.

I had heard that there was a site opposite city hall named Place Marie-Josephe Angelique. Most visitors do not know that Angelique was a black woman slave. The central core of the city burst into flames on April 10, 1734, destroying a hospital, convent, and forty-six homes. Angelique was captured, accused, tried, convicted, tortured, and hung in the public square on June 21, 1734. Tonight, on the front lawn, a towering, snow-dusted, glass-beaded Christmas tree was ablaze with twinkling lights.

Back home we drank cups of rum-spiked eggnog and called it a night. We were awakened by the *ding-donging* of the telephone.

"Don't answer," cautioned Bill.

"Why?" I asked.

"We don't know who it is," he whispered.

"There are only three people that know the number. Bell Canada, us, and New York," I confirmed. The ring died and surged back to life.

"Clifford, it's New York," she was calling from a pay phone. "Herb and I will visit Montreal on Thursday, December 1st," she announced. They would be traveling under the guise of a couple visiting Montreal. Herb would be crossing over. The intervening weeks had flown by.

"It was New York. She and Herb will arrive on Thursday, December 1st," I informed Bill.

"I hope he gets over," mused Bill. "How long is New York staying?" he asked

"We will find out later," I replied.

We informed our neighbors that we were expecting Stateside visitors. Bill and I were slightly apprehensive. We had grown familiar with each other's living habits and idiosyncrasies. Neither of us had shared living quarters with Herb or New York. I was less concerned than Bill due to my longer-standing relationship with Herb.

The next few days were a blur of house cleaning. I shopped at the Atwater Market for produce and meats and visited the liquor store for wines and spirits. There was an evening knock on our door. It was the wife from next door. She had a bucket of household cleaning supplies in hand.

"I've come to clean your kitchen and bathroom," she announced.

"It's all good." I spoke.

"Yeah, yeah, but not good enough for a visiting woman," she emphasized.

She scrubbed and buffed the bathtub, sink, and toilet. Hung fresh face cloths and towels and issued new scented bars of soap. She cleaned and spit-polished both fridge and stove and left with a laundry bag of sheets and other washables.

I thought that I had done all that. But the bright and sanitized surfaces gleamed otherwise.

CHAPTER EIGHT
# DAY OF CARGO

> *"Where you came from is gone. Where you thought you were going to never was there. And where you are is no good unless you can get away from it."*
>
> —Flannery O'Connor, *Wise Blood* (1952)

I hunkered down in the kitchen mixing seasoning for smothered creole pork chops, washing and chopping collard greens, peeling and squaring sweet potatoes for candied yams, regular potatoes for potato salad, and a mix for cast-iron-skillet cornbread. I loved being in the kitchen. The seasonings, marinades, and other fixings reverberated with distant childhood memories of apron-clad connections with mom and grandmother.

Bill set the table and opened a bottle of white and red wine.

Voices and footsteps echoed on the stairway, followed by a knock on the door. New York was ebullient and enthusiastic in her embrace. Herb was less so. He appeared weary and edgy. The anxiety and long bus ride, perhaps? We showed off the apartment. Herb dropped his suitcase and carry bag near his indicated army cot. I gathered up my sleeping bag and relinquished my cot to New York. I would be bunking on the sitting room sofa.

We sat for supper. All lavished praise on the culinary feast. We drank copious amounts of wine. Over coffee, I presented Herb with his Canadian identification documents. He tapped the papers, nodded, and smiled in appreciation. We moved to the sitting room, drank whiskey, and listened to jazz on the radio. All of us sensed that it was not the time to discuss weighty matters. I suggested a next day itinerary: touring Little Burgundy, lunch at Bens Deli, and the look-out atop Mount Royal.

New York and Bill retired. Herb remained in the sitting room with me. I noticed his shaking hands.

"It's good to be on foreign soil," he said.

"Glad you made it," I replied.

He sighed, embraced me, and said, "Tomorrow."

"Tomorrow," I replied.

Morning broke with the jingling sounds of cups. New York was preparing coffee. Herb was on the balcony scrutinizing St. Antoine Street. He appeared refreshed. Perhaps sleep had reduced the anxiety of successfully crossing over. The temporary surcease from the habitual glancing over the shoulder. "Don't look back. Something might be gaining on you," cautioned the legendary Satchel Paige.

"Good morning, cold in here," New York greeted.

"Our radiators have a severe case of the hesitation blues," I cracked.

"More like a case of the death row blues," she quipped.

Herb came in from the balcony. "Brrr, colder in here than outside," he whimpered.

"You'll feel different, once you've been outside longer," Bill assured.

New York's coffee elevated our body temperatures. She offered to make breakfast.

"Thanks, but we can chow down at the downstairs restaurant," I volunteered.

Lucille, resident waitress, greeted Bill and I. "Oh, I see you have relatives or friends," she exclaimed.

"Visiting friends," I said.

"Well, welcome to Montreal and my bailiwick. What will you folks have?" she asked. Lucille served us extra amounts of toast, scrambled eggs, pancakes, bacon, sausages, home fries, and *fèves au lard*—baked beans with lard. She flashed the 'shush' sign. "Don't tell my manager."

Stomachs satiated, we set out on the tour of Little Burgundy, Union United Church, Atwater Market, Negro Community Centre, Legion branch, and rhythm and blues and jazz clubs. We skipped lunch at Ben's and climbed the stairways up Mount Royal. The veil of snow was thick, lathery, obscuring the hallmarks of the city.

Back home, we ate Caribbean chicken patties, sliced mangoes, and stewed pigeon peas. Herb quickly switched the conversation to Africa. Montreal had always been thought of as our intermediate station on the underground railroad. Africa was to be our final depot. New York would be leaving tomorrow.

Over morning coffee, Herb handed me a handwritten list of mostly books about Africa. I left to visit a previously passed bookstore on Ste. Catherine Street—Argo Bookshop. The tiny shop resembled a Dickensian tableau. Creaking floorboards, floor to ceiling shelves, sagging under the weight of crisply new and aged books. The shop was the literary hub for aspiring writers and the imprint of small literary presses. John George—Mr. George—was a tall, soft-spoken, bulbous-nosed gentleman with a wispy tuft of white hair and a protruding stomach which stretched his suspenders and the buttons of his blue cardigan sweater. The shop boasted obscure local and out-of-print editions. Mr. George delighted in sleuthing out hard-to-find books. He filled my order but for two titles. The outstanding books would be ordered with an estimated arrival in one week.

I enquired about books by black Canadian authors. He fastidiously piled an assortment of volumes and suggested that I begin with Austin Clarke's novel *Survivors of the Crossing*. He provided a telephone contact for Alfie Roberts. Recommending his expertise in Caribbean, African, and black Canadian studies. Alfie hailed from the island of St. Vincent-Grenadine. He was a former cricket player and constabulary police officer and had attended political conferences in the Soviet Union and Cuba. I phoned Mr. Roberts that evening.

Alfie was welcoming, spouting reading guidance. He was a font of knowledge on trade unionism, West Indies federation, Pan-Africanism, and anti-colonialism struggles. He would afterwards recommend books about Quebec and Canadian topics. We would spend hours discussing our readings over the telephone.

Sometimes there were invites to his Goyer street apartment to greet and chat with visiting Caribbean writers from London, England: Derek Walcott, Wilson Harris, Samuel Selvon, Orlando Patterson, Andrew Salkey, Walter Rodney, George Lamming, Kamau Braithwaite, and C.L.R. James. I especially related to the themes of exiles, rootlessness, and alienation, whether coerced or self-imposed, expressed in the works of Lamming and Selvon.

We would, every Saturday morning, brave the blustery snows and winds. Alfie's weather-battered black fedora and billowing trench coat puffing our sails, propelling us down Ste. Catherine Street and thoroughfares on our maniacal Ahab quest. Harpooning rare and priceless discoveries of first edition catches of Africana. Argo Bookshop was always the first nautical outpost of our literary seafaring.

Words cannot describe our rummaging through the book bins of the Notre-Dame Street Salvation Army store and the exhilaration of discovering first editions of African

American Booker T. Washington's autobiography *Up From Slavery* ($1.50), Paul Laurence Dunbar's *Lyrics of a Lowly Life* (50 cents), and contemporaneous newspaper clippings of their travels and speeches tucked between pages. There were volumes from the historical societies of Ontario and Nova Scotia ($1.75) chronicling slavery in those respective Canadian provinces. Original proceedings of the Universal Negro Improvement League convention and speeches of the honorable Marcus Garvey in Montreal.

Mr. George's and Alfie's tutelage would motivate my acquisition of knowledge and expertise in book collecting that eventually resulted in a personal collection of three thousand rare and out-of-print volumes of African American, African, Caribbean, and Latin American books.

Regrettably, many of those musty, dusty English-language independent bookshops would eventually succumb to the predatory encroachment and corporealization of book chains, and the internecine language wars of Anglo dominance vs. Quebec nationalism.

I cradled the bag of Bob's suggested titles and set out for home. I heard brawling voices as I climbed the stairs. A French-speaking couple was having at it. Savory, ambrosial vapors streamed underneath our apartment door. Bill was in the kitchen. Herb was in the sitting room surrounded by copies of the *Montreal Star*, *The Gazette*, *La Presse*, and *Le Devoir*. He smiled and took the book bag.

Bill announced supper. Tidewater seafood chowder, cheese biscuits, creole tomato salad served with a chilled bottle of white wine. The meal was no doubt a homage to his childhood days in Virginia. The creole tomato salad was my contribution. He beamed in response to our hand clapping and finger licking.

"This is the kind of cooking that brought Virginia back into the union," claimed Herb.

"It's the kind of cuisine that kept poor black families united at the table of comity," bowed Bill.

"It was such wafting smells that made us kids abandon childhood games and scamper home," I offered. The drinks and conversation flowed into the late hours. We went to bed knowing that New York would be leaving in the morning. I awoke early and prepared coffee and toast. We said our goodbyes and Herb accompanied New York to the bus depot. Bill and I tidied the kitchen. Herb returned and requested that we join him in the sitting room.

"We need to talk about our plans," said Herb.

"We have to establish a routine that keeps us safe, anchored, and focused on getting to Africa. That means that we need to educate ourselves about the real Africa before getting there. I have put some thought into this." He paused, consulting his notepad.

"We could approach this by doing weekly theme-based discussions supported by guided questions. We could rotate facilitators, and we need to have structured time to check in on our mental health status. Being open and honest about the stresses of being away from home and the difficulties of adjusting to our new realities. How all of that can impact our living together and our personal relationships. I think that French language skills will be helpful here and in Africa. I am willing to assist with that instruction," he continued.

I nodded. Bill was stoic. Herb surveyed the room, looked at me, and continued. He broached the subject of security measures, agreed upon behaviors and practices that would keep self and others safe from detection, detainment, and deportation. Herb knew that he risked greater exposure due to his public profile and notoriety. The FBI dragnet would be broad and the manhunt more dogged in tracking him. We clearly had to be heedful of not drawing unnecessary attention to him. The beam of his celebrity would also make it difficult for us to remain in the shadows. We agreed not to discuss each other with outsiders, not to have unagreed-upon visitors, and expenditures and all future earnings belonging to the house. Herb would do house cleaning detail. Bill and I would do groceries and meals.

Herb sheepishly requested that we smoke our cigarettes on the balcony or off the premises. Bill cast a furtive glance and temporarily turned his back to the conversation. I consented on our behalf. Bill went out to take air.

"He will be alright," I said.

"That's not too much to ask. Is it?" Herb asked.

"Maybe too soon," I offered. "He will be alright," I repeated.

I busied myself in the kitchen preparing hamburgers, oven-baked fries, and a salad. Bill returned and set the table with beers. It was a surly meal. Bill was taciturn and ate with his head bowed. Herb quit the table. I plated and placed my burger in a warm oven and asked Bill to join me on a walk.

"Who does he think he is?" snapped Bill.

"He doesn't smoke," I reminded.

"He's got all these ideas about study sessions, routines, and discipline. Self-imposition. Dictatorial. He didn't even ask our opinion," he sputtered.

"You didn't voice any disagreements," I countered. "We no longer have the place to ourselves. You and I have learned to accommodate our preferences and idiosyncrasies. Things will be different going forward. We must talk out rather than act out our differences. Otherwise, we implode," I stressed.

He passed a cigarette.

"Well, we better smoke these before we get back inside," he said with a smile.

I consumed my hamburger and fries. Herb and Bill conversed in the sitting room. I closed the bedroom door, snuggled in my cot reading the Martiniquean, negritude adherent, Aimé Cesaire's *Discourse on Colonialism*.

## CHAPTER NINE

# GONNA BE A LONG NIGHT

*"Tote dat barge, lif' that bale."*
—Paul Robeson, Show Boat (1927)

Over morning coffee, we thumbed through the classified ads in the *Montreal Star* newspaper. There was an advertisement for seasonal workers at Simpsons department store and another for sales and promotion at Classic Bookstore on Ste. Catherine Street.

Bill insisted on applying for the book shop. I would have prized working with books. However, I relented. I did not want to risk further bruising his disposition. Bill gained employment at the book shop, and I was hired by Simpsons. I would be working in the men's stockroom along with seven other seasonal employees. We worked the overnight shift ensuring that all the menswear was adequately and neatly displayed for the morning, noontime, and holiday evening rush.

My supervisor, Alexei Kuznetsova, 71, was a short, adroitly attired, and aggrieved Russian émigré. Alexei was a shrivel of a man. He sucked his cigarettes to butt end and had yellow-stained fingers that complimented his tufts of golden hair. He was also afflicted with a congenital snort. He was a book lover and crossword puzzle enthusiast, and never failed to puzzle the Sunday *New York Times* crossword. Alexei was a tavern habitué. He took a liking to me. On weekends we would drink draft beer and talk books. He was my entrée into the world of Russian literature. Once, in discussion, I volunteered that Alexander Pushkin, father of modern Russian literature, was black.

"Impossible," snorted Alexei.

"No. It's true. His great grandfather Abram Petrovich Gannibal was a former African slave and later served as a general to Peter the Great," I insisted.

This was the extent of my Russian historical knowledge. The corrective nugget was courtesy of black bibliophile A.J. Rogers. It and other of his revelations had served us well in the trench warfare combatting the racist trivializing of our black achievements.

Alexei, after further research, days later admitted, "You were damn right. Leave it to the communists to Sovietize history."

Herb, Harvard philosopher, mathematician, and renowned scion of the civil rights movement, was holed up in a telephone cubicle soliciting subscriptions for *The Montreal Gazette* and washing dishes at a Chinese restaurant. He was washed out by day's end. I felt for Herb. It was much too dicey to benefit from his Bob credentials.

The ninth-floor warehouse at Simpsons department store was windowless and lined with narrow cubicles and shelves. The highest cubicles could only be reached by use of a clunky sliding ladder. We stacked the snazzy, practical, fashionable men's apparel on a four-wheel iron trolley and rode the freight elevator down to the main floor. The elevator had exposed cables and would hiccup, rattle, stall, and spasmodically plummet downwards. The climb upwards was equally capricious. The main floor men's department was all aglitter and razzle-dazzled with a simulated snow-cottoned floor, suspended ceiling holly and a lofty perfectly formed and decorated Christmas tree.

Standing sentinel was a laminated cardboard likeness of a hulking, predictably alabaster-faced, white bearded, and crimson-nosed Santa Claus—harbinger of yet another white Christmas. I smiled, recalling the quip of black comedian, Dick Gregory: "Ain't no red-dressed white man foolish enough to climb down no ghetto chimney, shouting ho, ho, ho, ho. And if he ain't, then Rudolph and the other reindeer damn well know better."

I would breakfast at Bens Deli in the wee hours of morning. The eatery would be raucous with the banter of early morning jazz musicians, cabaret entertainers, strippers, call girls, and cashmere-coated, tweed-suited, primed-for-work businessmen. I savored the early morning walk home; the wash of the dawn light, the still falling, taintless snow. The contrast of my homeward-bound, soft, muffled footsteps and the rustle of head-down passersby trudging to work.

The Christmas rush was frenetic. We worked overtime to keep the display floor supplied. Customers lined the sidewalk, roughing the winds, snow, and sleet. The lines down the street were even longer as people jostled to view the annual Ogilvy's mechanical Christmas window display. A wooden mill cranked in circles illuminated by little Christmas lights and a myriad of fantastic and fluffy creatures. Tomorrow would be the annual employee Christmas party—to be held at Magnan Tavern and Restaurant—which was celebrated for its succulent roast beef with fixings, beef ribs, and calamari.

Twenty-five of us gathered in a private dining room, squeezed amongst long tables and a Christmas tree bulging with secret Santa gifts. I was cheek-to-cheek with another seasonal employee. A petite, beguiling twenty-three-year-old white girl from Trenton, Ontario. She was a second-year student of social work at McGill University. Eleanor B. Ellie, she insisted, lived in a small apartment on De Maisonneuve at the corner of Wood Avenue.

Ellie was pleasant, chirpy, and curious. She had blue-pooled eyes and wavy cropped black hair. She was firm and shapely. We tossed our beers, gossiped, and exchanged life stories. That is, as much as I could truthfully divulge. She had a younger teenage brother. Her parents were civilian employees at Canadian Forces Base Trenton. Mom was a clinical social worker. Dad was a recreational specialist.

"May I have your number?" she asked.

"I don't have a phone," I lied.

She provided her address and number.

A laughable, mirthful, inebriated guest Santa slurred the gift list. I was handed a large bag brimming with colorful tissue papers disguising a smaller goodwill $150 Christmas bonus cheque and a copy of *Le Petit Prince*. The story of a young prince visiting various planets, Earth included, moralizing on themes of loneliness, friendship, love, and loss.

Later, Ellie and I shared a taxi. She suggested dropping me off as I lived nearer. I dodged that bullet by claiming that the longer route provided the opportunity for me to see where she lived.

Days later, I accepted an invite to accompany Bill to the Classic Bookstore Christmas party. Herb cautiously remained below the tracks. The Classic Bookstore Christmas party, in contrast, was a stand-up, napkin-wine-and-cheese, paper-cup, finger-food, and brainy affair. Bill and I stayed late assisting with the cleanup. We were rewarded with a block of Brie cheese, smoky bacon-wrapped sausages, and a box of Jacob's Cream Crackers.

Back home, Herb joined us for a bottle of wine, party leftovers, and Louis Armstrong's "Christmas in New Orleans" on cassette tape. I informed them of my encounter with Ellie and that we planned to lunch at the McGill University student union building. I quickly assured everyone that she had no knowledge of our residence, little or no particulars about me, nothing of them, and that I would keep it that way. Herb's unexpressed skepticism was nevertheless audible. We talked of Christmas holiday plans, and it was agreed that I would cook the meal, and Bill would purchase a small tree from the Salvation Army sidewalk sale.

I climbed McTavish to the student union building. A small group of sandal-clad Hare Krishna faithful, a non-migrant species, identifiable by their billowing, fiery orange saris, were perched ankle-deep in the mushy snow. Each had a single lock of hair with a vertical facial marking starting just below the hairline to nose tip. Some reverentially banged their tiny handheld cymbals and chanted the Krishna mantra. Others extended offering cups and pamphlets.

The student union was a grey three-story complex with large glass windows overlooking the McLennan library. The main floor was furnished with comfortable sofas, lounge chairs, and tables. There was a second-floor cafeteria and basement café called "The Alley." Offices, meeting rooms, and auditorium were located on the third floor.

The building walls were plastered with posters and graffiti championing Cuba Libre, Quebec Libre, Revolution Tranquille au Quebec, Black power, Women Power, Labor unionism, and African liberation. Leonard Cohen's voice could be heard above the din of flutes and guitars.

Ellie arrived looking preoccupied. I ordered two hot chocolates. She sat with her head down. I waited for her to speak.

"I am not sure about this," she said.

I was not sure about what she was not sure about. The weather? The political climate? Me? Us?

"I don't really know anything about you. You're really guarded and seem offended when I seek answers from you," she ventured.

"I am not offended, but don't know you well enough to answer some of your questions," I countered.

"This doesn't make for a good start. Maybe I should go," she pronounced.

"If you really think so," I agreed.

She thanked me for the hot chocolate and was gone.

The next few workdays were strained. We passed each other with a nod of awkward recognition. By the end of the week, she approached and suggested that we meet for lunch on Saturday. We met at the Swiss Hut on Sherbrooke near Park Avenue. A well-known eatery and drinking hole for hippies, draft dodgers, poets, pundits, gadflies, commies, and separatists—most likely in separate booths. They all gathered to scheme their schemes and generally thumb their noses at the dull ordinaries.

We selected a booth and ordered a pineapple pizza, beers, and talked beneath layered clouds of cigarette and marijuana fumes. The room was a welter of discordant sounds. It was almost impossible to hear each other over the din. Ellie leaned in and apologized for abruptly ending our previous get together. She had been nervous and overly cautious. I sought to soothe her anxieties by explaining that my hesitancy to be unknown or unseen by others had complicated the situation. That I, too, had never been involved in an intimate interracial relationship—not true. I also acknowledged that my risk-taking, unlike hers, was not juiced with concerns about friends or family.

"Thank you for saying that," she said.

"It's about where I come from. Race is electric. Heated. Everybody gets scorched. We all have our coded and protective armor—our early warning systems," I replied.

"To be truthful, my parents would never accept our relationship as anything other than friends, and I am not strong enough to withstand their disappointment or displeasure," she declared.

Silence ensued. She was tearful. I felt for her. My journey was strewn with so many turns, choices, and scar tissues that I was largely beyond concerns about what others thought about my choices. However, it was another reminder of how race can shut down possibilities.

"I understand," I assured her, and I did.

"I hope we can still see each other and do things together," she offered.

"We can and we should," I replied.

We gently squeezed hands, left our pizza untouched, downed our beers, and agreed that we were serious about our intent to do things together and we did. We dined frequently and attended many concerts. She introduced me to the Quebec and Canadian music and arts scene.

On our last meeting, we attended the National Ballet of Canada's performance of the *Nutcracker Suite* at Place des Arts. She went home for Christmas and the holiday snows covered her trail.

## Noel Noir

Simpsons posted their list of holiday workers being retained for full-time employment. My name was not on the list. Alexei explained that they were only retaining bilingual speakers.

*Relou*, I thought to myself—French for "sucks"—and turned my attention to preparations for our first Canadian Christmas.

Bill went to buy a tree from the Salvation Army sidewalk sale. His choice left a lot to be desired. But we made the perquisite fuss. We decked the tree and admired the twinkling lights. The scrawny specimen could barely support the weight of the angel star topper. We substituted a lightly crumpled aluminum foil star, Hallelujah to Alcan Canada! I had decided to go all out with a Cajun Christmas menu of appetizers, side dishes, main courses, and desserts, all of which required long hours in the kitchen with my trusted bottle of scotch. My appetizers consisted of Cajun spiced pecans, Cajun chicken dip, and spicy Cajun boiled peanuts complimented by side dishes of boiled shrimp pasta, Cajun oven fries, Cajun mashed potatoes, and southern greens with bacon. All blessed with a main course of crispy Cajun chicken, chicken and sausage gumbo, creole chili, cheesy shrimps, and grits, Cajun shrimp boil, one-pot jambalaya, and red beans and rice. Finished off with desserts of pecan pie bread pudding and banana pudding.

We were a long way from home and families. The three of us. We only had each other. Our shared struggle and uncertainties about our journey's end. I had been brought up to believe that food is the bridge that connects us to home and identity. Coming together, sharing food and tales is our most communal and binding ritual and I labored to honor that tradition. We chowed down in the glow of that spirit with laughter and affection.

It was a sense of Christmases past. Dad and me crossing the silver-coated Petal Bridge, axes on shoulders, climbing down the muddy and soggy embankment, and chopping away at the pyramid shaped balsam fir. Dad always granted me the final whack. Scattering balsamic scented wood chips and the thud of the tree trunk kissing the powdery dusting of Mississippi snow. Christmas is always inescapably about how we did it when we were young. Our beggarly living room tree evoked the ghost of Christmas smells drifting up my nostrils.

Later, we drank bourbon and exchanged gifts. Herb sadly informed us that New York's efforts to garner support for our leaving Canada for Africa had faltered.

Nineteen sixty-six was coming to its end. It seemed so long ago. But it had been little more than a month since Bill and I oarded the bus, with fear and trepidation, which only subsided with the Canadian border agent's cheery, "Welcome to Canada!" and the subsequent safe crossover of Herb. None of us had ever imagined being exiled in another country. It was not easy living with the anvil of fear of being hunted down and returned to the United States. I longed for my family. I hankered for the South. I idolized my losses.

## CHAPTER TEN

# ALL THAT JAZZ AND A CONVERGENCE OF POLITICAL CONSCIOUSNESS

*"It's not the notes you play, it's the notes you don't play."*

—Miles Davis (attributed)

*"There are notes between notes, you know."*

—Sarah Vaughn (attributed)

*"You blows who you is."*

—Louis Armstrong (attributed)

I first met Frank "Slim" Williams at the McGill Student Union Building. He was a black war resister from Chicago and an accomplished jazz musician studying music at McGill University. His wife, Catherine, was white and worked as a manager at the nearby Sherbrooke Street branch of the Canadian Imperial Bank of Commerce. Their marriage was on the rocks and would soon flounder. Frank "Slim" Williams was tall but not slim. His over-the-belt sagging girth was bracketed and supported by bright red suspenders. His hands were large with elongated fingers. Hence the moniker "Slim."

Frank was always dressed in black from his head to the end of his highly glossed black high-top shoes. His head was invariably crowned with an askew black beret. The poster child image for the quintessential jazz man. He would caress his upright double bass like jazz man Buddy Bolden's horn calling home his sheep. He once bowed me to tears as he sawed a version of Lester Young, and the Kansas City Six's take on "Pagin' the Devil."

He and Catherine lived in a large apartment atop McGregor Street. Four of us other black American war resisters frequently joined him for coffee, music, home food, and backyard tales from another country. We gathered to drink in the New Year. It was a long homesick session besotted with anger and resentment about American racism and exile. I left early, stopping to place a pay phone call to Ella Gaston in Hattiesburg, Mississippi. I wished her Happy New Year and asked her to convey best wishes to my family. I continued home to bring in the new year with Bill and Herb. We ate holiday leftovers, drank dark rum, embraced, and went to bed.

I had promised to join Frank "Slim" Williams to watch the New Year's Day Rose Bowl football game. I arrived at noon. Outside, a gaggle of people were engaged in head down conversation. There was an Urgence Santé ambulance, police vehicle, and a gray van on the scene. Its side and rear panels emblazoned with the insignia of the office of the coroner. Attendants wheeled a gurney bearing a burgundy blanket-wrapped corpse. The lanky and bulky figure had to be Frank. The landlord recognized me and explained that Catherine had earlier informed him that she was leaving, and that Frank would now be responsible for the apartment. Later, a downstairs tenant had called to complain about leaking water. The landlord had knocked and entered. Frank was submerged in a bathtub of red suds. The landlord assured me that he had notified Catherine. He granted me permission to enter the apartment to retrieve my copy of James Baldwin's *Notes of a Native Son*.

Frank's four-string upright double bass was mounted on its ebony wood stand. The dangling horsehair wooden bow standing sentinel. I recalled Frank saying that 'rest' notes are little symbols that tell the player to be silent for several beats and that the double bar symbol indicates the end of a piece. I plucked the string, and the dark, weightless, raspy, menacing vibration echoed my exit. I later spoke with a distraught Catherine. She told me that she had persistently, to no avail, prodded Slim to seek professional support. Langston Hughes' haiku poem "Suicide Note" came to mind "...The calm, cool face of the river asked me for a kiss...".

1967 was a giddy, insane year, commemorating the one hundredth anniversary of Canadian Confederation and Montreal as the site of Expo 67 (April 27 through October 29). The dream project was erected on two gigantic islands in the St. Lawrence River: Ninety pavilions representing one hundred and twenty-one governments and cultures. Fifty million Canadians and international visitors sang and danced to the theme of "Man and His World." Offering Montreal to the world and bringing the world to the city.

But it was a troubled world. The political climate in Quebec during the '60s had been tempestuous with the rise of Quebec nationalism, the raging Vietnam War, growing black resistance in the United States, political upheaval in Latin America, and in the Caribbean. Blacks in Montreal were growing more insistent about racism and some advocates of Quebec nationalism and independentists were seeing themselves in a similar light, as manifested in their rhetoric and struggle against Anglo-dominance and juxtaposition to the plight of blacks in the United States as expressed in Pierre Vallière's *Negres blancs d'Amérique* translated as *White Niggers of America*. This precept galvanized their efforts to contextualize their plight with the ever-growing decolonization and liberation movements in the former colonies.

I was enthused by this coalescence of progressive forces and the cultural flowering and diversity stemming from Expo 67. But I was not in a celebratory mood. I no longer had the companionship of Frank. The solemnity of his suicide and the absence of employment haunted my wakeful hours.

I devoted early morning hours to reading classified ads in search of entry level employment. "Workers needed. No experience necessary," announced the advertisement. It took some effort to locate the tucked-in and signless building off rue De La Gauchetière. The edifice looked shuttered except for the ajar front door. The narrow stairway was dark. The plastered walls were puckered and damp to the touch. Acme Printing Company was stenciled in Greek and English lettering. The shop was large, windowless, and darkly lit. I joined others lining the wall of the hopefuls. I was invited into a small cubicle and instructed on the principles of silk screen production. The mainstay of the operation was printing menus for small scale Chinese restaurateurs.

"The work can be hard and requires precision. The hours are from 6 a.m. to 6 p.m., Monday through Saturday. The pay is $6.50 per hour. Anatole will train you. If you're interested."

I was assigned a silk screen platform with a suspended wooden handle attached to a rubber block squeegee. Underneath was a secondary platform with a manual register to lock in and secure the plasticized menu sheet and a draining tray for residue ink. It was painstaking and laborious work. The first impression of temples and dragons required red paint thickly applied by brush. The second reverso impression highlighted menu items in black ink. Successful output required a smooth and flawless swipe of the squeegee. The sheets had to be carefully removed, transferred to racks, and dried by high velocity hot air fans. Days later my hands were blotched and raw from acetone and other toxic cleaning solvents. I asked to use gloves but was told that gloves would negatively impact the dexterity required to accomplish a smooth application of the squeegee. I suffered daily from nausea and loss of appetite.

I informed Bill and Herb that I would collect my pay on Friday and not return. I headed homeward, flush with my paltry paycheck.

The door of the Black Bottom Jazz Club was open. I went in to say hello. The owner, Chuck, greeted me as he swept the floor. "Just quit my job. It was filthy and making me ill," I told him.

"I can use a dishwasher," he announced.

"I cook too," I pointed out.

"Are you sure?" he asked.

"Sure, I am sure," I assured.

"Well, I can't afford no amateur-hour production. But the cook does get sick sometimes," he acknowledged.

I continued homeward and gleefully informed Bill and Herb of my new job of dishwasher and sometime cook. Dishwashing is a steamy, sudsy grind. But it was a living of sorts. However, I relished those rare opportunities to cook. Fried chicken wings are a finicky enterprise. I had dined many times on Black Bottom wings and found them tasty. Most versions of seasoned flour include salt, black pepper, paprika, and cayenne pepper. But it is the cornstarch and baking powder that guarantee a crispy and crunchy skin. I soaked and rinsed the wings in vinegar. Marinated the wings in buttermilk, paprika, kosher salt, black pepper, and tabasco sauce. I drained the wings. Rolled them in the seasoned flour. Each piece was placed on a wire rack and inserted in the fridge for two hours. This is a must. The coldness binds the batter to the chicken which prevents sogginess and sticking when the wings meet the sizzling oil. You need a combination of oil, butter, and fresh garlic for frying. Don't follow recipes that instruct you to turn the chicken once. I turn frequently, ensuring a fully cooked, golden hued, and crispy wing. I supplemented the regular menu of wings with sweet potato fries, fried okra, and wedges of cornbread.

The voices of patrons drifted above the kitchen pantry door with shouts of "Who is the new cook? He is a keeper."

Chuck, smiling broadly, stood in the kitchen doorway. "You're a keeper," he confirmed.

The Black Bottom kitchen would be my personal hitching post for the remainder of 1967. The pay was handy, under the table, tips plentiful, and the music righteous. The Black Bottom was an exciting but part-time job. But I needed more income. I saw an ad for working with children.

I enrolled in the in-service training program of the Jewish General Hospital Institute of Family and Community Psychiatry as a specialized educator on the children's psychiatric ward. The work provided another perspective on humans and psychological development, and its impact on the marginalized, voiceless, and largely stigmatized.

I continued the weekend dishwashing and sometime-cook job at the Black Bottom. Herb continued to work washing dishes and plotting our way to Africa. Bill was now bartending at the hip and stylish Sir Winston Churchill Pub on Crescent Street. He was truly enjoying the bohemian nightlife of Montreal: after work partying, alcoholic binges, and weed smoking. He routinely came home in the early hours of the morning. Bleary-eyed, exhausted, and wasted. He was also sloshed with homesickness. Herb was worried, hot under the collar, and disappointed.

Bill's mood went from bad to worse with news of his mother's death. He longed to go home. To be with his family. I would frequently visit the pub to provide support and remind him of the risk of attending the funeral. He had a photograph of his mother leaning against the bar mirror and cried as he served drinks. I can remember the many times that Bill, the bartender, had consoled his patrons. All was now downside-up. The regulars now comforting him. I would often return at last call and coax him homewards. Those were sad, tearful journeys along Ste. Catherine and down Guy to St. Antoine. All the while Herb was leaning on me to stabilize Bill, to mitigate the loose-lip risk associated with Bill's increased use of alcohol and weed. Bill, in turn, was vexatious with what he considered Herb's self-righteousness.

Herb was excited that plans were coming together for our possible departure to Africa and dreaded that Bill might be compromised and in no condition to manage the passage. He insisted on scheduling a meeting to sort out matters. Bill was not eager to discuss Africa with Herb. I convinced him to book-off sick and join us. It was a doomed encounter. Bill showed up late and was obviously under the influence. His speech was slurred. His head flopping as he nodded in and out of sleep. Herb left the table. I went to the bedroom, pulled back the sheets and guided Bill beneath the covers. I entered the bathroom. Sat on the lowered toilet seat and silently cried.

I knew that Bill, older than me, had more history and ghosts to vanquish. So, who was I to judge? "It was better not to judge the man who had gone down under an impossible burden. It was better to remember: Thou knowest this man's fall, but thou knowest not his wrasslin," wrote James Baldwin. I advised Herb that we should call it a night.

I walked over to the Black Bottom Jazz Club and returned at 2 a.m. Herb was asleep. Bill was gone. It was a sad breakfast club. The food went untouched. We drank our coffee in silence.

"I will find Bill later," I said.

"What's up with him?" asked Herb.

"You mean other than homesickness? The death of his mother?" I asked.

"Plans are shaping up for Africa. Do you think that he still wants to go?" asked Herb.

"I have no idea. I don't even know if he knows what he wants to do," I spoke.

"Do you still want to go?" he asked.

"Yes, and no," I responded.

His gaze was quizzical. "Well, you have to decide soon," replied Herb.

There was a sense of urgency, and it was a complicated plan. The Williams family, across the hall neighbors, had agreed to officially adopt Herb as a long lost and abandoned cousin. Gilding him with their family name and lineage. Herb would use this newly acquired status as a means of securing a legitimate Canadian passport. The Williams had other Nova Scotian family that would do the same for Bill and myself. All of which, to my calculations, appeared convoluted and dicey—a gambit which could lead to our discovery, deportation, and incarceration.

I promised to speak with Bill and provide answers for the two of us. I had sacrificed all by escaping to Canada. An unimagined distance and geographical divide between self and family. I longed to return. To get closer rather than farther away from beginnings. Neither route was certain, but Canada was closer to Mississippi. But how to get back and back to what? "It is not drawn on a map, true places never are," wrote Herman Melville.

I left for the Sir Winston Churchill Pub in search of Bill and was told that he had booked a room at the Drummond Street YMCA.

"Afternoon, Bill," I greeted.

He extended his hand. "I am not doing well. I need to get home. Not just because of my mother's death. I need to be home," he said through droplets of tears.

I looked away while he dried his eyes. *So do I*, I wanted to say. But did not for fear of compounding his yearning.

"I been talking to some people. They have experience getting people across the border. It will take some money. Can you make a loan?"

"I can make a loan but crossing the border, getting and staying home is not the same thing," I warned.

"Just asking. I haven't decided anything yet. How are things at the house?"

"Not the same without you. Herb is still hatching plans for Africa. He wants to know if we are still in."

"No way. Africa is not home. I am finding it difficult enough to live here."

I understood. There was no need to add that he found it difficult, or near impossible, for him and Herb to stay under the same roof.

"Will you be going?" he asked.

"I don't know," I said. "Are you working this evening?" I asked.

"Taking the day off," he replied.

"Good. Then you can let Herb know your decision at supper," I suggested and invited.

"No. I intend rooming at the YMCA. I won't be going back there. You can bring my belongings to me," he announced.

The finality of his pronouncement wobbled me. It portended a fundamental repositioning of not only what we had been but what we would no longer be to one another. I returned to the apartment.

Herb could see that I was rattled. "Did you find Bill?" he asked.

"Yes. But I think I was talking with Herman," I replied.

"What are you saying?" asked Herb.

"Oh, nothing. Displacement, longing, identity, home, not the motherland," I said.

"Are you saying that he is not going to Africa?"

"In short. Yes, and he is not returning to the apartment. He will be rooming at the YMCA."

Herb hung his head. "Has it to do with me?" he wanted to know.

"Yes, but it is much more labyrinthine than that." I sought to lessen the blow.

I decided to wait until tomorrow to disclose my decision not to go to Africa. We passed the evening reminiscing about better times. The future, for the moment, could wait. I ended the evening by assuring him that Bill would be alright. "It's not all necessarily about us. His emotional equilibrium requires separation and a quiet space to reassemble," I prophesied.

The following morning Herb and I walked the Lachine Canal. Sat on a bench and watched the rapids frothing above the rocks and beating down upon our ears with sounds of sombre menace. If time is running out, you do not have long to say something.

"I won't be going," I said.

"Very well," he replied, as he gently tapped my knee.

The two of us knew that there was so much more that was unsayable.

## Masquerades

Weeks later, early morning breakfast, Herb presented a duly certified declaration of adoption and application for a Canadian passport. Bob Moses, aka Herb Robinson, was now officially a bonafide long lost Nova Scotian cousin of the Williams family and certified Canadian.

Coretta Scott King, Professor Jim Torczner McGill University, and Fred at Place des Arts, Montreal. Mrs. King, although best known as the wife of Dr. Martin Luther King, Jr., was an accomplished musician and created her own legacy of social justice activism.

I left the apartment for my evening shift at the Jewish General Hospital. The children were raucous. Edna, age seven and autistic, was flapping, rocking, spinning, and ritualistically arranging and flipping toys. I took my break in the basement canteen. The Wayne and Shuster Comedy Hour was on the television screen. Knowlton Nash, Canadian broadcasting correspondent, interrupted the show at 6 p.m. to announce that Martin Luther King, Jr. had been assassinated in Memphis, Tennessee. All of us employees and patrons were stunned. My stomach convulsed and eyes teared up. I lifted the receiver of the canteen telephone and informed the head nurse that I was not feeling well and needed to go home. All eyes looked sideways or downward as I exited the building.

Our small black Zenith television screen was too minuscule for such a cataclysmic moment. Herb crossed the room and embraced me. He poured drinks and we cried as we watched the dominoes fall. City after city fractured and bursting into flames. Policemen and national guardsmen brutalizing, shooting black protesters, and looters without distinction. I walked uptown to the Sir Winston Churchill Pub in search of Bill. The same scenes were unfurling across multiple television screens. The patrons were anchored in silence. Bill swaddled me in a buddy hug. I felt the dampness of tears on my shoulder. "We knew that this would happen," he said. I nodded in reply.

"How is Herb handling this?" he wanted to know.

"A man of few words but visibly shaken," I offered.

Dreams such as Dr. King's had become nightmarish. It occurred to me that Mississippi, home, would forever be even farther away. "Perhaps home is not a place but simply an irrevocable condition," wrote James Baldwin. T.S. Eliot put it this way "home is where one starts from."

It should be of no surprise that James Earl Ray, King's assassin and America's most wanted fugitive, ended up in Canada after fleeing from the Missouri State penitentiary. Ray was serving a twenty-year sentence for armed robbery. He had hung out the previous summer in Montreal. Visiting Expo 67, grifting brothels, and rolling tourists. Post assassination, out of desperation, he sought refuge in Toronto. Surmising that an English-speaking province would be more fertile to secure a counterfeit Canadian passport. His plan was to fly to Europe and finally Africa where he felt he could earn a living as a mercenary. No easy feat, given that there was a massive manhunt underway. The FBI and RCMP discovered that he had obtained false credentials and a Canadian passport, and Scotland Yard detectives arrested him at the London airport on June 8.

Herb had, during the intervening weeks, obtained his passport and had booked his passage. His ticket had to be rescheduled due to the swirling chatter amongst beer-drinking black baggage workers that there was increased RCMP surveillance and passport scrutiny at the Dorval Airport. It was later apparent that the increased surveillance was due to the manhunt for James Earl Ray. Herb could not risk traveling at the time. Herb said his goodbyes two weeks later. I wished him a safe journey and waved from the balcony as the taxi drove away.

That evening, next morning, and the following day, I walked the streets and paced the floor anticipating the horrifying American and Canadian newscasts that Herb, long sought-after iconic civil rights activist, had been apprehended at Dorval airport—to say nothing of the attendant jeopardy for Bill and myself. My mounting anxiety subsided when Sylvester Williams knocked on the door and informed me that Herb, without incident, had safely disembarked in Tanzania, East Africa. I called to reassure Bill.

Herb (Bob) had been the seminal influence in the maturation of the younger Fred Anderson and the older Clifford Gaston. I had seemingly always been in his gravitational orbit. Our roads had now diverged. I drank a bottle of Ben Afnam—an Algerian red wine—and luxuriated in the velvety-bluesy tones of Joe Williams crooning "Just Friends."

I decided, days later, to personalize my surroundings. I refurbished the apartment: Salvation Army-issued sofa, chairs, bed, kitchen utensils, bookshelves for my growing collection, and assorted variegated plants.

A week later, the personnel director of the Jewish General Hospital was updating and validating high school leaving certificates and professional accreditation. She had been very patient, despite her many entreaties, that she needed my documents. She had truly been lenient with my obfuscations and procrastination. Time had run out.

"I can't wait any longer, Clifford. Something is not right, and I am doubtful whether you can do anything to make it right." She was correct. There was no way that I could produce the documents. The FBI had alerted all state and federal agencies not to issue, without their approval, any document request names listed on their draft resister registry.

"I regret having to lose you, but you leave me no choice. Here is your cheque for salary owed. I will only advise your coworkers that you decided to move on. Good luck, Clifford."

It was not an unsurprising thunderclap. I would need to find other means of supplementing my Black Bottom Jazz Club income.

# PART III

## CHAPTER ELEVEN
# ABEYANCE

> "What's left is palimpsest—one memory
> bleeding into another, overwriting it."
>
> —Natasha Trethewey, *Thrall: Poems*,
> Houghton Mifflin Harcourt (2012)

Time is voracious, disobedient, and incessant. Bill and I had to keep moving. He was now attending Sir George Williams University and working in the library stacks. I was employed at Browser's Bookshop and occupying a third floor two-and-a-half apartment on Milton Street at Saint Urbain. Like Bill, I was attending the same university. The school featured a day and evening division and was unique in its cultural/racial diversity and working-class demographics.

Three significant events ensued. I met *J*. She was an undergraduate student pursuing a degree in the fine arts. We eventually decided to live together and relocated to larger quarters on Durocher Street near Pine Avenue. I now had ample accommodations for my growing book collection. *J* was white, demure, and dismissive of her beauty. I soon trusted her enough to make a full disclosure about my background and circumstances in Canada.

### Home Comes to Montreal

On my twenty-first birthday, I was awakened by a knock at the door. I was stupefied. It was my sisters, Ruby and Thelma, and Lisa, my eleven-year-old niece, Ruby's daughter. How had this happened? My contacts had been limited to calls from pay phones and never, ever had I divulged my whereabouts.

"Happy birthday, Fred!" they whooped. 'Fred' sounded extraterrestrial and did not elicit a Pavlovian response. They sensed my bewilderment, smiled, and said, "Happy birthday, Clifford."

"Come in, what a surprise!" I yelped. We chatted over coffee and croissants.

"Well look at you, Fred—I mean, Clifford."

"No. Look at you guys. I hardly recognize you and Lisa looks just like Ruby," I countered.

"Dad, Mary, and Sheliah send their love and can't wait to see pictures of you."

They clicked away and showed recent pictures of themselves, dad, and extended members of the southern tribe. We spoke reverentially of bygone days, vanishing family, relatives, friends, and schoolmates.

"Look at us, forgetting our manners. It's so wonderful to meet *J* and thank you for making this happen." I glanced in the direction of *J*.

"She goes over and beyond to ensure that I am cared for," I allowed, for now. They were now teary-eyed and relieved that their baby brother was seemingly healthy and safe.

Being in another country was a unique and quirky experience for them. Especially the diversity and francophone characteristics. Five days later, it was time to go. I exhorted them to be heedful of who they talked to about my whereabouts. It had, in the end, been a compensatory gathering tinged with the recognition of disremembered shared history and irreclaimable bygone days.

*J*, anticipating my vexation, apologized for the ambush but feared that prior knowledge would have resulted in my shutting down the plan. I was concerned and remained so going forward that this trip could potentially be the breadcrumbs that would lead to my ruin.

However, *J* would never intentionally put me at risk. I would marry her a year later as Clifford Gaston and later again as Fred Anderson. We would eventually part ways. But I remain eternally grateful and in awe of the courage she displayed. Risking all to keep me safe.

Another significant event was the four-day Montreal Congress of Black Writers convened on the campus of McGill University (October 11 through 14, 1968). Montreal author David Austin described the Congress as "a landmark shift in Canadian black consciousness. The moment at which Montreal became central to international black radical politics." International black intellectuals, authors and radical luminaries would be in attendance such as C.L.R. James and Walter Rodney. I was especially excited that SNCC veterans Stokely Carmichael and James Forman would be there. I salivated in anticipation of the moment of our reunification.

I approached the two with wide-eyed surprise during the meet and greet.

"Fred, is that you?" they exclaimed. I noticed the puzzlement on the faces of some of my black Canadian friends. I knew that I must, sooner than later, provide an explanation of who Fred is. I hurriedly yanked Carmichael and Forman aside and put them in the know. We would later enjoy drinks and chat in their hotel room.

It was my first in-person fellowship that whiffed of home and my thirst for authenticity. I quaffed every gesture and turn of phrase. End of Congress, we exchanged syrupy embraces

Stokely Carmichael at the Montreal Congress of Black Writers, McGill University, 1968. (Photo courtesy of the author)

and prolonged goodbyes. My euphoria was eventually dampened by consideration of the associated risks of our rendezvous.

The environment of 1968 Montreal was fiery and combustible due to strikes by police officers, teachers, taxi drivers, and student organizations, all intersecting with activities of anti-poverty groups, the influence of the U.S. black power movement, and Quebec *indépendantistes*. The Congress of Black Writers added even more heat to the political climate. The provincial and federal governments were agitated and surveilling all of these forces and their activities. The galvanizing scope of the Congress and my expanding connections with local black leaders, hauled me out of the shadows and into the glare of activism in black community activities. Looking back, I shake like a leaf at the thought of my recklessness. I had been so devout in my schemes and stratagems to avoid exposing my identity and whereabouts. Thinking and rethinking every potential mishap. Attending the Black Writers Congress was tantamount to being a moth to the flame. However, I was so desperate and starved for any opportunity at genuine connection to home and with those who had been central to my involvement in the civil rights movement.

It was a portal that would, however momentarily, lift the burden of being somebody else and allowed me to be, however fleetingly, Fred Anderson. I reasoned, although risky, the moment was what I required to move forward.

## Some Stars Shine Less Brightly

> *"Small, disconnected facts, if you take note of them, have a way of becoming connected."*
>
> —Walker Percy, *The Thanatos Syndrome* (1987)

Charles Saunders was a Vietnam War draft dodger, age 24, white, and from the red clay hills of rural Georgia. Sarah, his wife, cooked the most wonderful meals. The kind of spread which called to mind our down-home compliment: "Girl, you must have stirred that with your foot."

I first met the couple at the aforementioned Swiss Hut on Sherbrooke Street. Sarah was substantial and diffident. Charles was diminutive and voluble. We exchanged pleasantries. He leapfrogged from not returning to the U.S., his dislike of Canada, and his resolve to find a way to Cuba. It was all Fidel-this and Che-that. He wanted to know if I knew anything about Cuba.

"Only what I have read," I replied. "My itch is to eventually return to Mississippi," I added.

"That's a god-awful place," he retorted. I kept my silence. "Do you know the location of the Cuban Embassy?" he wanted to know.

"On McGregor Avenue in the vicinity of the Montreal General Hospital," I told him.

Months later, an overwrought Sarah entered the Swiss Hut and pulled me aside. Charles had met with two men who had guaranteed documents for safe passage to Cuba. Yesterday, the three had arranged a late evening meeting at the chalet atop Mount Royal.

They promised, the next day, to drive him to the Cuban Embassy. Charles had not returned.

Had I heard from him? Did I have knowledge of the two men?

I answered in the negative and promised to ask around. Perhaps some of the Swiss Hut regulars had heard or noticed something.

Two weeks later she received a letter, postmarked from Leavenworth Military Prison, Kansas, U.S. Charles had been entrapped, deported, and sentenced to the Leavenworth military stockade.

Days later, we said our goodbyes and she boarded a flight bound for Georgia.

### Unwilled

*"My Memory stammers, but my soul is a witness"*

—James Baldwin, *The Evidence of Things Not Seen* (1985)

My grandmother once told me that you had to walk more responsibly after you had witnessed something. It was her way of saying that the past and the present collide. "Much,

much, much has been blotted out," wrote James Baldwin in *No Name in the Street*.

I do remember meeting Wendy and Patrick Quarry. Patrick was employed at N.D.G. Photo, located on Phillips Square, in the heart of downtown Montreal. He encouraged and instructed me in the process and practice of photography. Wendy was a wispy blonde from Toronto, Ontario. Recently returned from a stretch of CUSO volunteer service in Ghana, West Africa. She was in Montreal to assume charge of Quebec CUSO—overseeing promotion, recruitment, and orientation.

Wendy had the appearance of being wind-churned. Whizzing from one activity to another: parenting, international development excursions, real estate, and broadcast journalism. Traditional CUSO training modules were premised on volunteers grasping the historical backgrounds and cultural cosmology of their area assignments. Wendy concluded that a more engaged and enriching volunteer experience would benefit from a values clarification approach—ways in which 'self' potentially inhibits understanding of other spaces and peoples. The two of us no longer recollect how we came to know of the other. Perhaps, it was the Black Writers Congress. She is tolerably sure of having been there. It could be that she had been windswept into Browser's Bookshop. Wendy, ill or good winds aside, offered the assignment of developing, and delivering, the training curriculum.

That is how Bill and I came to meet weekly with a group of twelve CUSO volunteers. Soon to depart for their area assignments in Africa. We gathered for two-hour sessions in the sitting room of my Durocher Street apartment. Bill and I authored reading and discussion guides for Paulo Freire, *Pedagogy of the Oppressed*; Albert Memmi, *The Colonizer and the Colonized*; Ayi Kwei Armah, *The Beautiful Ones Are Not Yet Born*; Camara Laye, *The Radiance of the King*; Chinua Achebe, *Things Fall Apart*; Frantz Fanon, *The Wretched of the*

*Earth*; Walter Rodney, *How Europe Underdeveloped Africa*; Harold Cardinal, *The Unjust Society: The Tragedy of Canada's Indians*; Eldridge Cleaver, *Soul on Ice*; and Roch Carrier, *La Guerre, Yes Sir*. Most of the volunteers thoroughly enjoyed the sessions. A few disgruntled, had no time "for this self-actualizing approach." Meanwhile, Wendy was devoting more and more time to real estate and journalism. She pulled off a covert, on-camera exposé about neglect and abuse in elder care facilities. It was a stellar piece of journalism laying bare some of the fault-lines and practices that would years later, account for the unimaginable, and the inordinate numbers of Covid-19 deaths in senior care facilities. Her radio and television broadcasts were garnering a larger audience. Wendy was now in need of childcare support, and I needed the money. So, I took charge, as a full-time babysitter for her two young boys. It was a baffling arrangement. Only a sense of mutual desperation could have led us down this path. Suffice it to say that the boys survived.

## CHAPTER TWELVE
# SNOW OF A DIFFERENT KIND

> *"Until the lions have their historians, tales of the hunt shall always glorify the hunter."*
>
> —African proverb

The year 1969 saw the onset of a seemingly unfamiliar weather event in Montreal. White-punched computer cards and other documents snowed and fluttered down from the nineth floor windows of Sir George Williams University computer centre. Orange flames and black smoke billowed; the papers blanketing the sidewalks and street. White and black student protesters wheezed and coughed as they stumbled and raced towards fresh air. Enraged white bystanders flashed the Nazi salute and fanned the flames with shouts of "Let the Niggers Burn."

The smoke, flames, and hurled racist vitriol sounded the doleful knell of the fourteen-day sit-in, then the largest student occupation in Canadian history. The asthmatic conclusion of what came to be dubbed The Sir George Williams University Affair, Computer Party, or Riot. Resulting in two million dollars of destruction of equipment and the rising tide of black consciousness in Quebec and internationally.

On April 28, 1968, six Caribbean students lodged a complaint with the office of Dean of Students, accusing biology

Professor Perry Anderson of biased grading, and demanded the creation of a representative committee to hold hearings into the matter. The university administration, after waning hopes that the conflict would fade away after ten months of inaction, conceded to the necessity of striking an investigative committee. The composition of the committee, absent student body input, unsurprisingly, proved contentious. Some black professorial advisors resigned in protest. Two hundred frustrated, angry, protesting students walked out of the hearings and occupied the ninth-floor computer center. Black students, along with mostly allied white students, submitted a list of demands.

The students assumed, or were led to believe, that there was an agreement in principle that: a more representative hearing committee would be struck; students would not destroy computers or property; there was to be no police intervention; and students would abandon the occupation. Notwithstanding swirling rumors that the administration had already relinquished authority to the police, many of the protesters abandoned the occupation. However, subsequent clarification revealed that there was no principle in agreement but rather a vague consideration to entertain student demands.

The remaining students were now convinced that the administration was stalling and in collusion with the police. The protestors countered by erecting barricades on the seventh-floor escalators, locking down elevators, and disabling phones.

The Montreal police riot squad stormed the building and dismantled the barricades, ending the occupation on February 11, 1969. But not before a fire erupted, and in the ensuing chaos, ninety-seven arrests were made of black and allied white students. Thus ended the day with a different kind of snow.

Professor Perry Anderson had been placed on paid leave for the duration of the standoff. The administration deemed the allegation of biased grading baseless, and he was reinstated the following day.

The judicial outcome for the arrested protestors was less conciliatory. They had been hauled off to jail. The identified black leaders were dealt harsh sentences, ranging from three to ten months' imprisonment and deportation in some instances. White allied protestors received lesser sentences or probation.

The black students never stood a snowball's chance in hell. Local and national media, the business class, and other tycoons drove the narrative of the "others": black foreign students hellbent on destruction, willfully and maliciously undermining Canadian values, and the tenets of multiculturalism and inclusiveness. Black and white students insisted that reckless police actions led to the destruction. The 'othering' narrative insisted that they and they alone were responsible for the conflagration and destruction.

It was a heated and conflicted citizenry. Ever-growing segments of the black population grew angry with the newcomers—black foreign students disturbing the hard earned "racial calm." Such phrases of consent emboldened the media to become even more hyperbolic and acerbically jingoistic. It was all too familiar. It was not the South, but the slumbering, horned, hunchback beast of xenophobia rearing its head, licking its tongue, and igniting the smoldering embers of pluralistic myopia. A short-sightedness that led all levels of governance to underestimate the potency of inequity and perceived racism, even as blacks and other marginalized constituencies had been consistently denouncing structural racism. The Sir George Williams University Affair made news around the world and transformed Montreal's black community.

Senate Block. Ottawa, Ontario, July 2017. A private viewing of the National Film Board of Canada's *Night Floor* (2015) documentary about a troubled chapter in Concordia University's history where black students occupy the Hall building to protest institutionalized racism. Left to right: Fred Anderson, Senator Anne Cools, and the late Dr. Clarence Bayne, founder of the Black Theater Workshop and so many other black cultural initiatives. Senator Anne Cools, longest serving member of the Senate of Canada (1984-2018), was a central figure in the occupation, sentenced to four months in jail and pardoned in 1981. (Photo courtesy of Pat Dillon)

Bill and I thought it was best not to be in the spotlight cast by these events. I did attend some meetings of local community support groups. I attempted to boost their efforts to shift the narrative and broaden support. I anonymously authored a petition and two advocacy articles in black community newspapers.

It was at one of these meetings that I met economics professor Clarence Bayne. He and several other black faculty members had, unsuccessfully, made attempts to moderate and educate the administration on the nature of the crisis and best strategies to achieve a satisfactory outcome. (Parenthetically, as the calendar turns the page on 2021, the provincial government of Quebec continues its flat earth narrative that systemic racism does not exist in Quebec.) Ironically, Graham Carr, president and vice-chancellor, of Concordia University, fifty years later, on October 28, 2022, acknowledged and apologized for the "stark manifestation of institutional racism reflected in the manner in which the university mishandled events."

The dust settled and I continued to pursue my university studies at Sir George Williams University (later, Concordia University)—a heavy concentration of advanced history, literature seminars, and psychology. My portfolio of essays and short stories gained approval for entry into two highly coveted advanced writing seminars.

CHAPTER THIRTEEN

# STATE OF APPREHENDED INSURRECTION

*"You don't need to accept everything as true; you only have to accept it as necessary."*

—Franz Kafka, The Trial (1969)

The 1970s had consequential beginnings. Military tanks rolled down the streets of Montreal. Thousands of soldiers patrolled and manned strategic locations. Prime Minister Pierre Elliott Trudeau had invoked the War Measures Act. Historically, the Act gave the government full powers during wartime to censor and suppress communications; to arrest, detain, and deport people without charges or trial; to control transportation, trade, and manufacturing; and to seize property. Canada had only previously resorted to the War Measures Act during two periods of its history: World War I and World War II. Never in peacetime. Until what became known as the October Crisis of 1970.

The Crisis, though a singular marker, cannot be understood as a singular event. It was the culmination of an elongated series of terrorist attacks by the Front de Libération du Québec (FLQ). A militant wing of Quebec's independence movement. The FLQ were responsible for more than two hundred bombings. Including mailboxes, major department stores, the Montreal Stock Exchange, government buildings—notably the provincial Department of Labour—and of targeting city mayors, the Premier of the province, and anglophone corporate elites. Munitions sites were burglarized and there were dozens of bank robberies between 1963 and 1970. Many were injured and six killed.

The FLQ felt emboldened to use an even more confrontational approach in pursuit of its goals. James Cross, British Trade Minister to Canada, was abducted from his Montreal residence on October 5, 1970. The FLQ issued an ultimatum to the Quebec government that Cross would be freed in exchange for the release of twenty-three FLQ "political prisoners," the broadcast and publication of the FLQ manifesto, $500,000 in gold, and safe passage to Cuba or Algeria. The Quebec government was given twenty-four hours to comply.

The provincial government rejected the ultimatum but acquiesced to the publication. CKAC radio broadcasted the FLQ manifesto on October 6. The station also received threats that Cross would be killed should the government fail to meet their other demands. Jérôme Choquette, provincial justice minister, announced on October 7 that he was available to negotiate. Meanwhile, the FLQ garnered national and worldwide recognition as a result of the broadcast of their manifesto and demands aired on the major CBC English network and French-language Radio Canada.

However, the FLQ grew impatient and raised the ante after the Quebec government refused to negotiate. Pierre Laporte, Quebec Minister of Labour, was kidnapped on October 10. The die had been cast. Prime Minister Pierre Elliott Trudeau invoked the War Measures Act on October 16.

Events turned deadly on October 17. The body of Pierre Laporte was discovered in the trunk of a green Chevrolet Biscayne near the airport in Saint Hubert, Quebec. By November 2, the provincial and federal governments jointly announced a $150,000 reward for information leading to the arrest of the abductors.

Meantime, there was intense police and military interrogations of the usual suspects. This resulted in narrowing the dragnet.

Police, military, and other operatives surrounded the suspected location of an FLQ cell on December 3. Negotiations resulted in the release of the British Trade Commissioner, James Cross, and assurances that the FLQ would be granted safe passage to Cuba. Five Front de Libération du Québec members, on December 4, boarded a flight to Cuba.

Military withdrawal from Quebec took place on December 24, 1970. Federal Justice Minister John Turner issued his War Measures report on February 3, 1971:

497 arrested. 62 charges. 32 retained without bail. 435 released.

Herman and I, fearful of being fortuitously entrapped, had decided to lay low and watch events unfold through the media. *J* and I suspended our university studies. She occupied herself doing watercolors and oil paint sketches. She had just recently been awarded a handsome fine arts endowment which bolstered our finances. I busied myself writing poetry and short stories.

The Provincial and Federal government had carried the day. "Just watch me," Prime Minister Pierre Elliott Trudeau had declared.

We are still watching. It is impossible not to sense that the events of October 5 through December 28, 1970 continue to reverberate and define the interactions between French-speaking and English-speaking Quebec, and Canada. Edictally, every politician, provincial or federal, without regard to party affiliation, examines deeply rooted issues contextually, with reference to its implications for Canadians and the Quebec nation.

## Medicinal

> "...Darkening the light and blotting out the sun;
> Go thou, my incense, upwards from the hearth,
> And ask the gods to pardon this clear flame."
>
> —Henry David Thoreau, *Smoke* (1843)

In the fall of 1971, Ann and Lance Evoy settled in Montreal. The couple came from Oil Springs, Ontario. The site of North America's first commercial oil well and home to the Oil Museum of Canada. Lance and his family have a long, rich, and distinguished heritage in Oil Springs. I recently enquired of him if my memory was correct, that his dad, and his dad's dad, had served as receiving station operators in the oil industry. He wrote back in the affirmative and offered that his great grandfather, Richard, came to Oil Springs in 1860 and was part of the oil boom, drilling a successful gusher well that produced over 3,000 barrels per day. He ended up, he continued, reinvesting most of his wealth in drilling dry holes and dying poor in 1888. Lance reminded me that there are still modern-day oil producers in Oil Springs, Ontario. We often spoke of visiting Oil Springs together. Not too late. Perhaps.

Ann and Lance had just recently completed a two-year assignment as CUSO volunteers in Sierra Leone, West Africa. Wendy had decided to move on, and Lance was tagged to assume oversight of CUSO Quebec's recruitment and orientation. Bill and I were retained to continue the orientation workshops. Lance and I grew to respect and trust each other. There is no better friend.

1971 was also the year that I joined with Professor Clarence Bayne, Dr. Yussuf Naim Kly, Grace Basso, Joy Sitahal, and others to establish the National Black Coalition of Canada Research Institute in Montreal. Bayne served as director, and I, as assistant director, oversaw the history division.

The National Black Coalition of Canada came into being in 1969. Shortly after the computer centre occupation at Sir George Williams University. I remain, to this day, perplexed as to how Professor Bayne, in his Trinidadian, gatling-gun cadence, convinced me to loan my three-thousand volume book collection to the institute! The institute quickly became the place to be. A contingent of local black artists painted the environment with historical and culturally vibrant wall murals. It can be said that one of the seminal legacies of the institute was its galvanizing and mentoring of a large sector of black youth. Many of whom continue to serve in contemporary agencies and organizations. Our jazz workshops, black poetry seminars and readings, history symposiums, and performance art nights were well attended and generated media coverage. The administration of Dawson College granted credits to students attending our seminars. Our media department developed black audiovisual content and conducted oral history interviews. Dr. Clarence Bayne was the leading force for so many creations of some of the most groundbreaking cultural initiatives at the center of black culture in Montreal, Quebec, and Canada. Especially the Black Theatre Workshop. We had a long-time partnership and friendship. It was more than troubling and sad to receive the announcement of his death on September 1, 2024. We bickered back and forth over installments of this memoir and his insistence that I needed to include this or that moment of significance. Sometimes the stars align and makes others shine brighter. That was the sparkling arch of his ascendancy. *Memoria infinita* Clarence.

Ruben Francois—"Ruben Black Snow Goat"—was one of the local black poets that read from his published and new poems at the research institute. Age eighteen, he, and his family fled Haiti to New York to escape the terror regime of Haitian dictator "Papa Doc" François Duvalier. He joined up

Dr. Clarence Bayne at Thanksgiving meal
at the home of Pat Dillon, 2020. (Photo courtesy of Pat Dillon)

with the New York Black Panther chapter and got into some difficulty with the police. Fearing further police harassment and induction into American military service, he emigrated, four years later, to Montreal. He became a familiar downtown sight—reading his poems in cafés, bars, coffee shops, and on the sidewalks. He scrounged a livelihood from washing dishes and the generosity of well-wishers.

I remember well the day. It was the morning of the 4th of July. I walked from the Institute to purchase books at Classic Bookstore. Ste. Catherine Street is always crowded at all hours. I noticed Ruben, near Classic Bookstore, chatting with an acquaintance. He waved and, with monkish style, lowered himself to the sidewalk, surrounded himself with volumes of his poetry, doused himself with gasoline, and lit the match. I, along with other onlookers, emitted sounds of awe and horror. The ambulance transported him to the Montreal General

Hospital where he was found to be suffering from first-degree burns on eighty percent of his body and not expected to live. He survived, in agony, for nearly three weeks.

Why Ruben? Did the date of July 4th hold symbolic meaning? What of the Buddhist-like self-immolation? Why in front of the bookstore? Some speculate a scorned lover narrative, or that he was intent on a mission to bring into focus man's inhumanity to man. All we are left with is his reported deathbed declaration to his attending nurse: "I did it for nothing." Which could be read to mean nothing, or too many things to be particular about.

"Misery won't touch you gentle. It always leaves its thumbprints on you; sometimes it leaves them for others to see, sometimes for nobody but you to know of," wrote Haitian author Edwidge Danticat.

The Institute flamed out in 1974. We got word that the National Black Coalition of Canada was undergoing a change of leadership at the national and provincial levels and intended on mandating a new management of the institute. Some national-level delegates viewed this as a hostile takeover in the making and opposed it. Professor Bayne, myself, and others, in the dead of night, backed a truck up to the rear entrance of the Institute, boxed up my book collection, and returned them to my apartment.

Remarkably, not a single volume was missing or soiled. Later in 1974, our original grouping morphed into the Black Studies Centre (Quebec).

The late Roy States, National Black Coalition of Canada secretary, transferred the Institute's archive to our keeping.

## Stories Don't Tell Themselves

> *"Just because you're paranoid doesn't mean they aren't after you."*
>
> —Joseph Heller, *Catch 22* (1961)

My efforts in the creative writing seminars were gaining notice. It was a small, culturally diverse class of students. I distinctly recall that the St. Vincentian Montreal novelist H. Nigel Thomas was among my classmates. Professor Abraham Ram was the saddest and loneliest character that I had ever encountered. I think it had something to do with having grown up a Jew with literary ambitions in the generation of Mordecai Richler, Leonard Cohen, and other Montreal Jewish *literati* and judging his achievements as less than theirs. Although, he did eventually author and publish a haunting autobiographical trilogy of his childhood years: *Noise of Singing* (1975), *Dark Cave* (1977), and *Once in the Woods* (1982).

We would have long alcohol-hazed sessions in the seventh-floor faculty club, as the bartender poured scotch and he, in turn, poured over my literary submissions. He broached the idea of editing and publishing an anthology of class writings. *Outset*, the collection, was published in 1973, featuring my short story and works by other students.

The story generated public interest, and I was invited for an interview on a CJAD radio morning show hosted by Hana Gartner. She was impressed with the short story depiction of the lifestyle of a Mississippi rural black farmer and his mother and grandmother.

"But tell me about your youth and growing up in the South," she interjected.

I steered the conversation back to the narrative of the short story.

"How did you come to write so well of this farmer? Is it autobiographical?" she interrupted.

"Incidentally," I replied.

"I sense a reluctance to talk about yourself," she announced.

"I prefer, as do some writers, to focus on the work," I emphasized.

The interview did not go well.

I did not want to further expose details about my identity or previous life. Cloak and dagger stirrings were afoot. I suspected that I was being spied upon. An edgy feeling about the same unfamiliar white car on my street at specific times of morning and night. The peculiar behavior of the black gentleman that joined me for coffee, over three consecutive days, in the university cafeteria. There was no lack of empty tables!

"Good morning," was all that he said and scanned the pages of *The Georgian*—the student newspaper. I finished my coffee and left for my writing workshop. He immediately got up and disappeared and reappeared the next morning.

Days later, *J* got a phone call requesting that she meet with the dean of the Fine Arts department. The dean informed her that an agent from the Royal Canadian Mounted Police (RCMP) had enquired about her and had been told that students' files were confidential. *J* was infuriated and concerned. We knew it was only a matter of time before the circle was squared. Especially, days later, when the neighbor across the hall informed *J* that an RCMP agent had knocked on her door and sought information about her.

*J* continued with school. I retreated to the apartment. Not answering the phone, furtively peering out of windows, and going for brief walks in the evening. Darting periscoped glances backwards and forwards for operatives lurking in the shadows. Bill had not noticed any unusual attention. He agreed that the events increased the urgency for obtaining assistance in legalizing our status in the country. He shared the name of a lawyer. The lawyer insisted that I had to reclaim my identity and apply for entry via the immigration process. He undertook to explore avenues to circumvent the FBI edict of not honoring requests to release school or birth records without disclosure and their consent.

Days later, I discovered a handwritten note in our mailbox. It was from Professor Ram.

*"Where are you, Clifford? I been trying to reach you. I have good news, call, or come to my office,"* he wrote. I did not reply.

I received another letter addressed to Clifford Gaston, embossed with the insignia of Sir George Williams University, dated May 30, 1973:

*Dear Mr. Gaston:*
*I am pleased to inform you that you have been awarded The Board of Governors Medal for Creative Work in the Literary Arts. This medal is awarded annually, when merited, to the student giving evidence of independent work outside the classroom of outstanding ability in creative expression.*

*This medal will be presented to you at the Convocation ceremony on June 10, 1973. Please contact Miss Valerie Richardson at 879-4235 for particulars concerning your gown and tickets.*

*May I extend to you my personal congratulations on being awarded this medal.*
*Yours very truly,*
*Kenneth D. Adams*
*Registrar*

I had no intention of attending. I called the number and lied. "I will unfortunately be out of town. Is it possible to send a representative?" I asked.

"Oh my, you must be so disappointed not to be present at such a distinguishing moment. Give me the name of your

Medal awarded under the name of childhood friend Clifford Gaston. Disappointing that I could not transfer to Fred Anderson. Nevertheless, a weighted reminder of how we were and always will be linked and how I lived for eleven years under a borrowed name.

stand-in and instruct him or her to contact me to conclude the arrangements," she agreed.

Jack Hannan, a fellow writer, and former colleague at Browser's Bookshop, attended the ceremony and collected the medal. The sleuths seemingly receded deeper into conspiratorial shadows. My radar, nevertheless, continued twirling and fanning the heat at the nape of my neck. Eventually, in 1974, Lance Evoy and I grew weary of the delimiting language and underlying cultural imperatives of international development discourse. We founded the Intercultural Development Education Project (IDEP) and shifted our focus to designing and implementing intercultural education modules for the Montreal Teachers Association (MTA) and the Provincial Association of Protestant Teachers (PAPT). I am no longer sure why IDEP came to an end.

Lance soldiered on with colleagues to create Third Avenue Resource Centre. The name is suggestive of a third option for comprehending and tackling social and economic justice issues in the community.

Many years later, in 1993, I would join Lance and others to establish The Institute in Management and Community Development as part of Concordia University's Centre of Continuing Education. The Institute was brought to fruition through our collaborative efforts with community-based groups.

Our popular University of the Streets Café featured a series of public conversations convened in cafés and public spaces across the city. Over the course of fifteen years our seminal Summer Program attracted 12,000 community workers and activists from across the globe to Loyola Campus for an annual week of accredited reflection and training symposiums. The Institute also pioneered an accredited diploma program in community economic development.

## CHAPTER FOURTEEN
# A BLUES FOR CLIFFORD

> *"By the pricking of my thumbs,*
> *Something wicked this way comes.*
> *[Knocking]*
> *Open locks,*
> *Whoever knocks!"*
>
> —William Shakespeare, *Macbeth* (4.1.44-49)

Hockey Night in Canada. *J* and I went to supper at La Bodega on Park Avenue. We dined on platters of Shrimp Valencia and downed carafes of sangria. The boisterous patrons stood and cheered at every Canadiens' goal or near miss. It was not to be.

A sombre mood dampened the *joie de vivre* of Montreal on the morning of the ninth of May. The National Hockey League's Buffalo Sabres had defeated the Montreal Canadiens in the semi-finals. Advancing to the 1975 Stanley Cup finals. The early morning bistro crowd sipped coffee in sullen silence. I paid for my croissant, café au lait, and headed for the offices of the Cote des Neiges Black Community Association. I was now the coordinator of youth development initiatives and a contributing editor to the *Black Voice* newspaper. I put in a long day finishing a grant proposal to convene a weeklong Montreal black youth symposium.

*J* devoted the early evening to cleaning easels, inventorying, and rearranging paint supplies. I hammered out an editorial piece for the *Black Voice*. Later, we told jokes, snacked on assorted cheeses with Jacob's cream crackers, downed a bottle of wine, and called it a night.

We awoke to an early morning hammering on the door. Two trench-coat clad gentlemen flashed Royal Canadian Mounted Police badges.

"Is your name Clifford Gaston?" the taller agent asked. *J* was now at my side.

"May we come in?" asked the smaller.

"Yes," *J* replied. We led them to the sitting room.

"Nice library," remarked the taller. I was about to say thank you had not *J* interrupted.

"Yes, it is. Thank you for noticing," offered *J*.

"What is this about?" I asked.

"You are Clifford Gaston?" he asked again.

"Yes, he is," said *J*.

"We are asking him," the taller one asserted.

"Yes, I am Clifford Gaston," I assured.

"We are assigned to the RCMP immigration detachment. We are following up on an FBI inquiry about your status in Canada," the taller one announced.

"Where were you born?" asked the smaller one.

"Truro, Nova Scotia," I replied.

"I guess we must have the wrong Clifford Gaston." The two stood, looked at each other, and left.

How had that happened? Professor Bayne and I, back in the days of the NBCC Research Institute, had smelled a skunk in the woodpile. The pungency was now astringent.

I looked at *J*. Her face was florid red, and her cheeks were hot to the touch. I was breathing in and out. Struggling to regulate my emotions. Neither of us were sold on the idea that they had stumbled upon "the wrong Clifford Gaston."

We agreed that the first order of business was to immediately inform Bernard Mergler—a well-known progressive attorney who specialized in political cases.

"Move. Move right now and come to my office first thing tomorrow morning," he commanded.

We contacted and informed Lance. He was agreeable to our storing furniture in his basement. *J* called a trusted friend. She quickly arrived and assisted with boxing books. She also arranged for storage space in the basement of her parents' West Island home. She also bravely agreed that we could bunk down at her place for the next few days.

We arrived early for the appointment with my lawyer. He was not yet in. He arrived shortly afterwards. He introduced me to his articling student, Juanita Westmoreland-Traoré—later to become the first black judge in the history of Quebec as well as the first black dean of a law school in Canada. "Wait here," he said.

He entered his office and returned with an envelope in hand.

"Let's go." He pointed down the street. It was obvious that he'd rather not discuss matters in his office. He handed over the envelope. It contained a certified copy of my birth certificate. Issued by the Mississippi State Bureau of birth records.

"How did you get this?" I asked.

"Don't ask," he replied.

"You two need to leave the country. Remarry and re-enter Canada as Mrs. and Mr. Fred Anderson. Go immediately to immigration and apply for landed immigrant status. You need to be fully truthful on your declaration. Any falsehood will render your application void and result in immediate deportation. Your marriage allows you to remain in the country until your application is either approved or rejected. Complete your application and present yourself to the RCMP detachment and ask if their agents have been looking for you. Call me upon completion of the process."

I called Lance and told him of the plan. He informed me that the agents had visited his home. They knew that our furniture was stored in his basement. So much for "the wrong Clifford Gaston" bunk.

I called Wendy. She and Patrick were now living in a wooden renovated elementary school in the small village of Mansonville, located in the Eastern townships of Quebec and adjacent to the United States and Canadian border near North Troy, Vermont.

*J* placed a call to her friend and was advised that we should not return to her place. The RCMP agents had visited her and aggressively inquired about our whereabouts. I frantically called Wendy and insisted we needed a plan.

"Don't worry. Just get here," she pleaded.

We were desperate for lodging. Errol and Joy Sitahal had a place on Lambert-Closse Street, near the Montreal Forum. They took us in. Errol went out to purchase beer.

"I am certain that they are parked across the street," he warned.

"What gives?" puzzled his wife.

"I don't know. They are obviously not ready to take me in," I surmised. "The clock is against us. We gotta move, like now," I advised *J*.

I launched an SOS flare to Wendy. "Coming tonight," I announced.

Errol called for a Diamond Taxi. "Downtown," I told the driver. "Turn here and wait on the side street," I instructed. He palmed the fare, and we entered the Mansfield Tavern, exited the rear door, jumped back into the taxi, and traveled to the bus depot. We purchased two tickets and traveled to Mansonville, Quebec.

The bus pulled up to the Mansonville crossroad restaurant featuring its life-size rocket on the launch pad. Seemingly poised to explore unknown galaxies. Wendy exited her car.

"Get in," she breathlessly exhorted. We huddled around the glowing embers of their pot-bellied wooden stove.

We would be leaving tomorrow morning for North Troy, Vermont. Wendy had arranged the marriage ceremony with a local justice of the peace. "We need to get in and out without delay," Wendy reminded.

The Canada-United States border is the longest unguarded border between two countries. The boundary is known to be unpatrolled for long unpredictable stretches—only requiring that visitors report to the nearest customs post. You can take your chances. Keep going and risk not being apprehended by hit-or-miss patrollers. Risky were the cards that we had been dealt. Into the breach was our only available option. Captivity meant the jig was up. The crash and burn of all my sacrifices and emotional investments in exile. North Troy is a mere six kilometers south of Mansonville, psychologically, interminable by stealth.

Patrick stoked the dying embers and added wood to the fire. No one spoke. Wendy and Patrick climbed the ladder to bed. *J* and I went for a walk in the veil of darkness. We could hear, in the distance, the bark-howl of the wolves. We embraced, tightly squeezed hands, and returned for a fitful sleep. Wendy came down and gifted us two of her sedatives.

I awoke to a chilled cabin and the wafting scent of caramelized nutty coffee. Patrick had built the fire and was scrambling eggs and toasting bread. We gobbled the coffee. The eggs and toast went untouched. We eased out under a hazy morning sky and self-imposed silence pierced by sounds of crunching gravel as the vehicle rumbled down rock strewn roads. Wendy was at the wheel, Patrick in the passenger seat, *J* and I in the rear. A sign read "report to the nearest custom post." We disregarded and plowed ahead.

"Get down," admonished Patrick. I lowered my body to the floorboard of the car.

Crossing the bridge into North Troy, a phalanx of U.S. police patrol cars, sirens blaring behind us. We were paralytic with fear. We veered to the emergency road shoulder. The convoy zoomed past in pursuit of the truck ahead! If stopped and questioned, I had only Lance's Canadian Social Insurance Card as claim of identity.

Shortly thereafter, *J* tapped my head.

"You can get up," Wendy exhaled. I unfolded my aching limbs and read a sign announcing that we were entering the Township of North Troy, Vermont. We continued down Main Street, seeing the prominently displayed sign for the office of the justice of peace.

A grey haired, robed gentleman welcomed us, and speedily officiated the wedding ceremony. He poured glasses of wine. *J* and I signed the certificate. Wendy and Patrick signed on the witness line. The justice of the peace affixed the seal.

We approached the Canadian border, presented our credentials, and were waved across.

Back at the Mansonville cabin, Patrick, trembling hands, uncorked the wine.

"Holy shit!" screamed Wendy. The four of us erupted in giddy and liberating laughter.

*J* and I went for a walk underneath the canopy of the darkness. Illuminated by the sparkle of aggregated stars. We gazed upwards and thanked our lucky stars. The inkiness of the night shrouded us as we re-entered the cabin. We drank the remainder of the wine and drifted down the slopes of an inebriated sleep. I could hear *J*'s spasmodic sobbing and felt the wetness of her tears. I knew then, as always, that I truly valued and loved her. Her unimaginable fealty astounded me.

Come early morning, Wendy drove us back to Montreal and wheeled into the front entrance of the Immigration Centre.

"Good luck guys," she said, and waved goodbye.

"A friend gathers all the pieces and gives them back in the right order," wrote Toni Morrison. That was Wendy.

We entered, took a number, and queued up for the next two hours. Our number was called, and we warily made our way to cubicle #3 and presented our documents.

"Mr. and Mrs. Anderson?" he asked.

"That's right," we replied, in unison.

"Is this one of those marriages of convenience?" he wanted to know.

"Love at first sight," I assured.

"Your papers appear to be in good order. Let's begin the application process," he invited. "Have you been to Canada prior to this date?" he asked.

The voice of my lawyer was pinging: *Don't lie.* "Yes," I told the clerk, as he checked boxes and made notes.

"Did you ever work during your previous visits to Canada?" he continued.

*Remember, don't lie,* the voice reinforced. "Yes," I declared.

His pen halted and lifted from the application form.

"That's illegal. I am required to suspend your application," he thundered.

"I was only trying to be totally honest with my answers," I assured.

He looked me in the eyes. Lowered his head for what seemed like forever. His pen rapidly tapping the form. He returned his gaze and emitted an elongated sigh.

"Mr. Anderson, I misunderstood your previous answer. My apology," he smiled. He signed and stamped the landed immigrant status card.

"Good luck to the two of you," he said, extending his hand.

"All the best to you," I greeted. And that was that. An unfathomable process in these post-9/11 and pandemic times.

*J* and I immediately, as instructed by my attorney, crossed over to the RCMP immigration detachment.

"How can I be of help to you?" asked the officer.

"My name is Clifford Gaston. I understand that you might be looking for me," I volunteered as that was the name that occasioned their early-morning knock at our door.

"Give me a minute, sir." He scanned the database on his computer.

"You are mistaken, sir. No record of you here," he confirmed.

We left. I called the lawyer and assured him that the journey and return had gone as planned.

"What about the RCMP immigration detachment?" he wanted to know.

"No record regarding me," I said.

"As I suspected. They were likely members of the subversive division. But they will never admit to that," he surmised.

"Congratulations. Get some rest and come to my office on Monday. There remains much work to be done to reconcile the histories of Clifford Gaston and Fred Anderson, before fully reclaiming your identity," he asserted.

We needed a place to stay—a new home for new beginnings. The generosity of friends provided temporary lodging while *J* scoured the newspapers in search of vacancies. We finally settled for an upper level seven-room flat on Jeanne Mance Street. In the heart of a Portuguese district.

We trudged our sleep deprived bodies up the stairway and slept for hours. I kept my Monday appointment with lawyer Mergler. He presented a stack of legal affidavits with a photo of my image paperclipped to the upper left-hand corner of each. He required that I visit each workplace or institution that I had been associated with as Clifford Gaston and secure their signature. Their signing was legal attestation that the appended photograph of Fred Anderson was the same subject that each had previously known as Clifford Gaston. The affidavits would authorize my attorney to file a request for the reconciliation and filing of employment, academic, and other institutional records under the name of Fred Anderson.

The exercise, though far from comfortable, went remarkably well. All were perplexed but left unasked: "What compelled you to assume the identity of another person?" Those that I thought deserving got unasked for answers. Regrettably, Sir George Williams University administrators could not transfer to the name of Fred Anderson the 1973 Board of Governors Medal awarded to Clifford Gaston for Excellence in Literary Expressions. The Board of Governors, I was told, is recognized as an autonomous entity, and as such, could approve my request. It appeared too hazardous to pursue the matter with the Board of Governors.

Attorney Mergler refused to accept a penny for his services.

The revenants of Fred Anderson were not easily interred. There were some that felt wrongfully deceived, betrayed, or wounded. No explanation or mea culpa would ever be sufficient to assuage their sense of moral outrage.

Still, to this day and I dare say when I lay dying: there will be some turning-the-corner moments of long-ago acquaintances, hailing, "Is that you, Clifford Gaston?" Sometimes, it occasions a hitching in my throat that falters, short of becoming audible. Not anymore, I remind myself and choke the urge. My favorite color has always been blue. The color associated with the blues. During the black "great migration" traveling blacks hopped buses, trains, hitched rides, or sometimes walked miles. Their guitar strumming and lyrical blues were the "keys to the highway," wrote Angela Davis. Blue expressions of the "jagged grains" of life's experience, echoed James Baldwin. Across blue highways and briar patches of Mississippi and snows of Canada, Clifford Gaston has and will always be my traveling companion.

CHAPTER FIFTEEN
# A DREAM DEFERRED

*"You might as well answer the door, my child, the truth is furiously knocking."*

—Lucille Clifton, *Good Woman: Poems and a Memoir, 1969-1980*

"What happens to a dream deferred?" asked African American poet Langston Hughes. "Does it dry up like a raisin in the sun? Or fester like a sore—And then run? Maybe it just sags like a heavy load...." The poem does not offer any solutions for prorogued dreams. Only tentative but potentially explosive musings. Sometimes the weight of the question, the clamour of emotions, the alignment of the personal and the political, insist on specificity.

I received, on January 7, 1977, an official summons to attend my Canadian citizenship ceremony. Well, not mine alone, but a group ceremony. I—we would be tested on twenty questions about the rights and responsibilities of Canadians and Canada's history, geography, economy, government, laws, and symbols. It had been a long-anticipated event. I found the stately Beaver Hall building and was ushered into the testing room. Stared at the twenty questions. Gulped air and relaxed. I knew the answers. We were led into an antechamber and individually told that we had successfully—or not—completed the exam. Handed a copy of the oath of citizenship, song sheet for "O Canada" and marched into a grand chamber with a raised dais. Flanked by a Canadian flag and the flag of the Province of Quebec, a robed citizenship judge entered. We stood as he administered the oath of citizenship: "I affirm that I will be faithful and bear allegiance to Her Majesty Queen Elizabeth the Second, Queen of Canada, Heirs and Successors, and that I will faithfully observe the laws of Canada and fulfil my duties as a Canadian citizen." We then sang the national anthem to the accompaniment of a scratchy recording: "O Canada, our home and native land! . . .." Congratulations were exchanged and out I went into the snows of 1050 Beaver Hall Street. I was, in the words of the gospel song: "Free at last, thank god almighty, free at last." No longer the dreaded nightmares of being ensnared in chains. Yanked away by slave patrollers and returned to bondage. The ceremony brought me one step closer to my get-out-of-jail-free card and passage to Mississippi. Days later, my Certificate of Canadian Citizenship arrived. I must say, on examination, that it bore an uncanny resemblance to the counterfeit one which Bill and I purchased back in 1966.

On January 21, 1977, U.S. President Jimmy Carter, in a convergence of probabilities, granted an unconditional pardon to hundreds of thousands of men who had evaded the draft during the Vietnam War. The long hoped-for dream of going home had arrived. "Every Southerner eventually comes home," Truman Capote said, "even if it's in a box." But eleven exiled years later, exactly what did *home* look like or feel like? So much of *home* was now Canada. Could I recover the *home* of yesteryears? Mississippi poet Natasha Trethewey, in her poem entitled *Theories of Time and Space*, wrote, "You can get there from here, though there's no going home. Everywhere you go will be somewhere you've never been. . .the photograph—who you were—will be waiting when you return." Perhaps. Another fellow southerner, Albert Murray, wrote of the bitterness and joy of the going home experience in his classic memoir *South to a Very Old Place*: going home, he writes, "has probably always had as much if not more to do with people as with landmarks and place names and locations on maps and mileage charts."

Yet I longed for it all. People, landmarks, place names, locations, and the ticking odometer that reconnects the dots between the living and the dead. What might have been and the still possible. I phoned my sisters and agreed that August was a more propitious time to visit Ohio, Hattiesburg, and to make the return drive with dad to Akron.

I boarded the flight with a scheduled brief stopover in Philadelphia. The U.S. customs agent scrolled and laconically consulted his computer screen.

"What is the nature of your visit, sir?"

"Family," I replied.

"Nationality?" he asked.

"Canadian," I replied.

"May I see your travel documentation?"

I gave up my Canadian passport. "It says here that you were born in the United States."

Correct, I confirmed.

"Well, in the future, you must, when asked, assert that your nationality is American. Otherwise, you will be denied entry," he bellowed. "Please accompany the agent," he indicated. I was certain that his computer search had marked me among the listing of President Jimmy Carter's pardoned Vietnam War resisters and that I was being singled out for nuance value. "Where did you say you're from?"

"Hattiesburg, Mississippi," I repeated. He surveyed the map.

"Where exactly is that?" he sighed.

"Ninety miles south of the state capitol of Jackson," I stressed.

Herbert Anderson (dad) and Fred, Akron, Ohio.
(Photo courtesy of Gary Anderson)

"It's not on my map," he feigned. Forty-five minutes later, "Wait, there it is, welcome home," he smirked. Pound of flesh exacted. Mission accomplished. Expenses incurred. I had missed my connecting flight. I trudged to the reservation desk and booked a later flight. I called my sisters—omitting details—and advised them of my alternate flight and time of arrival in Akron, Ohio.

Nephew Gary, Mary's son, stood at the arrival gate. His broad smile obscured by tumbling tears. "I better get you to the house. Your sisters Ruby, Thelma, Sheliah, and Mary are beside themselves." He was tall and bulky. Nothing like the dinky boy that Mary had carried away to Ohio. He steered the car leftwards on to Roslyn Avenue. The street was a sea of people. Music blared. I could barely see my sisters waving from the front porch. There were *Welcome Home* banners and colored lights flashing. The inside was adorned with similar banners and balloons. All my longed-for foods were lavishly displayed across many tables. The backyard overflowed with family, friends, and neighbors.

Mary was on rewind. Repeating, "Fred, Fred, Fred. Just look at you boy." Ruby stroked my head. Baby sister Sheliah intermittently squealed, "Look at Mr. Canada." Unknown nieces and grinning nephews jumped on and off my knees with harmonized greetings of "Uncle Fred from Canada." The sing-song thread of conversations: "Do you remember when?" The blues-gospel call and response of "I remember when." Albert Murray's proven prescience. Home was about the people. Bloodlines. Intuited half sentences. The sagacity of the nod, lifted brow, eye roll or the tonal qualifications of 'um-hum.' The southern gracing of food.

## My Kingdom for an Ark

*"There's too much blank sky where a tree once stood."*
—Jesmyn Ward, *Sing, Unburied, Sing* (2017)

We awoke in the dark hours of the early morning to the hovering steam of black coffee, buttered biscuits, and thoughts of driving south to Hattiesburg. Mary forewarned that Newman Quarters was enfeebled. Families dispersed. The flooding waters of the Leaf and Mississippi rivers had reclaimed the land. A few indomitable stalwarts had stood their ground "...just like a tree standing by the waters. I shall not be moved...." We arrived at cockcrow. "Be prepared," said Mary, as she wheeled onto Lee Street. I owly-eyed the flooded eviscerations of the proving grounds of my youthful aspirations: the family home at 326 Lee Street. Front porch twisted like a pretzel. The once habitable innards now compacted match sticks of wood pilings. 116 Lee Street: the homestead of my grandparents. The big house. Conquered. The tall bracing undergirding stilts succumbed to silt. Mt. Bethel Baptist Church knee-bowed to devilish destruction. Pews to dust. The collapsed pulpit. The bone-dry, shoulder-high baptismal pool. No longer capable of cleansing the soiled wings of fallen angels or slaking the redemptive seeking thirst of parched sinful souls. The mildewed, creosote-scented floorboards, clacked beneath my feet.

Fred Anderson and the late Voncile Gaston-Burkett, sister of childhood friend Clifford Gaston, in Hattiesburg, Mississippi, July 16, 2016. (Photo courtesy of James Donald)

Distended cabinets and drawers. Scattered hymnals, verses, and blemished funeral brochures. The final resting place of birth and death records. "Ashes to ashes, dust to dust." I reconceived the Sunday school class and a small boy's recitation of the shortest verse in the bible. "Jesus wept." I wept.

We walked, Mary leading the way, for a foreigner at home. The Inn. The site of the murder of Cousin Sammy. Gone. No longer a whiff of gunpowder residue or blood-saturated corpse. Gone. The site of the heat-seeking projectiles of Sammy's blasted hopes and my irreparable trauma. Erased. Mississippi author, Jesmyn Ward, wrote in *Men We Reaped*, "Men's bodies litter my family history. The pain of the women they left behind pulls them back from the beyond, makes them appear as ghosts. In death, they transcend the circumstances of the place that I love and hate all at once and become supernatural." It all reminded me of a Toni Morrison anecdote about searching for one of her early childhood homes. She drew a crude but cute map and asked her architect son to render a more precise version. She googled the image and was awestricken. "There's nothing there. Not even a street. There are trees. It's not like it's dilapidated—it's gone," she exclaimed.

Mary drove through the corroded gates of River Avenue Cemetery. The laneways had been flushed away. Trees twisted and uprooted. Some graves no longer six feet under but levitated and slushed open by the waters. "All water has a perfect memory and is forever trying to get back to where it was," wrote Toni Morrison. Perhaps it was this ancestral resorption of the waters that brought me back to these beginnings. We could not find the grave of mom. I did stumble across a fenced-in plot. Headstone still erect. "In memory of Private First Class, Clifford Gaston, Vietnam." I had not known. Stars in waiting, hopeful of roster assignment on the Hattiesburg Black Sox baseball team. Inseparable childhood friends. My namesake in exile. I knelt and looked upwards until Mary hauled me away.

"Ground Zero": Reckoning: resting site of Clifford Gaston.
(Photo courtesy of RM)

Damon Thomas Anderson (son) and Fred.
This book is dedicated to Damon.

We drove to see a relocated and greyed Aunt Lula. Her gold-crowned tooth still glinting family and resiliency. She pursed her snub-nosed pistol and accompanied us to the flood-ravaged cemetery and, like a Sherpa guide, led us to the grave of mom. It was as if in that moment, the waters surrendered claim on the land, and the restored roots twinned my grief with the aroma of spearmint chewing gum, hog killings, fresh cut flowers, the glint of green tinted bottles, and quilting tales. We returned to Aunt Lula's new house. She laid the table with evocative childhood foods and afterwards styled Mary's hair. I was again, instantaneously, the small boy sweeping up sheared locks from her beauty parlor floor. I reimagined her reprimanding and cautioning her patrons to be heedful of young ears. Lula, after mom's death, was the keeper of our grief and holder of our hopes. She waved goodbye from her front porch. It was a weighty leave-taking. Mary was crying. I dared not look back. It was time to see dad.

Dad was now living with his wife, Mrs. Alberta, in the East Jerusalem Quarters. It would be unusual seeing him with someone other than mom and elsewhere than 326 Lee Street. Mrs. Alberta was sitting on the screened front porch. She bounced up and held the door open. "Well, look here. Come on in Mary and Fred. Boy you sure look just like Herbert. Your dad's been crying for hours. He kept asking, 'Where are they? How come he's not here yet?' I reminded him that y'all probably revisiting Newman Quarters. He blubbered like a baby. Fred, that man has been on bended knee for years. Praying every night that God see fit to bring you home. Ending his blessing of the food with and God please bless Fred. I told him that he better save some of the tears for when you get here. Herbert. They are here!" she bellowed.

"As God is my witness. I been telling everybody and anybody that would listen that I would not be going to heaven or below until I set eyes again upon you, boy. Thank you, Mary, for driving him to Hattiesburg," he uttered through gushing tears. He extended his hand, and pulled me into a full embrace. I could feel the quiver of his rib cage.

"I love you dad," I whispered. He led us to the back porch gallery. The table was arranged with bowls, spoons, and ice cream scoops. I straightaway caught sight of the frosted burlap-covered hand churning, wooden, ice cream maker. A flood of memories breached my inner dam. The trace of soupy tears, calling to mind of just how much this moment, and other such moments, had sustained me. The Sunday-after-church ice cream. The little boy, butt cold, anchoring the bucket. A sweat-drenched dad cranking the handle. The same succoring memory as I endured harassment in the Hattiesburg City and Issaquena County jails. Into the woods to fell the best-of-the-best Christmas tree. He skillfully stringing straw chairs and the artistry of weaving intricately patterned cane bottom chairs. The richness of his fluffed coffee cakes. The swift lift-off and arc of his quilt-scrapped long-tailed kites. The whittled expressive wood figurines and chinaberry tree limbed windblown instruments.

Mrs. Alberta scooped bowls of ice creams. There is something sensual and maddeningly ephemeral about the melt of the first spoonful. I recalled, within days of my arrival in Montreal, the antique shop window display of an aged wooden hand cranked ice cream maker and instinctively understood why I had made the purchase without regard to price.

"Well, you ladies can talk. I am going walking with Fred," he announced. He stopped and greeted every porch and knocked on some doors. Always haranguing: "Remember my boy, Fred. Told you he would be able to come back home someday," clinched with a prideful smile. He had visibly grown tired. We stopped and perched on the steps of Morning Star Baptist Church.

"It was so special of you to remember and crank the ice cream. I remember it all, dad. The digging and drying of peanuts. Husking and savoring the salty, crunchy taste. All this, and so much more. The work of your hands."

"From one peanut farmer to another, it was my prayers and President Jimmy Carter that brought you home," he quipped.

"I thought this day would never come. Mrs. Ella would regularly tell me of those that had died in my absence. I dreaded the eventuality of hearing your name," I sighed.

"Well, I was reassured when your sisters Thelma and Ruby spoke of their visit. But I stopped the talk. Because I didn't want to know your whereabouts. I had always been able to answer the visiting FBI: I don't know where he is. But God bless Fred. Boy, you've done some things. Been some places. Seen some things. You coming back home for good?" He was the first of the family to give air to their unasked longings.

"I am not sure dad," I sighed. "You have been a good husband and provider. A solid dad," I added.

We returned to the house and thanked Mrs. Alberta for her hospitality. It was evident that she loved dad and took good care of him. I would always, after dad's death, call her from Canada and see her on each Hattiesburg visit.

It was now Sunday morning. Mary and I arrived at the relocated iteration of Mt. Bethel Baptist Church. I gazed upon the reinstalled original cornerstone. Etched in granite, the names of Henry Johnson, my grandfather, and Uncle Charles Anderson as two of the original founders. The pastor acknowledged returnees from near and far. All stood. I felt like the prodigal son returned. A matronly deaconess stood and spoke, "I just want the old, especially the young, to know and remember that we use to have some hard times down here. We were in trouble. And Maggie's and Herbert's son, Fred, stood up." Applause. I remembered that pride goeth before the fall. But, nevertheless, allowed myself to be momentarily warmed by the recognition. The choir burst into a medley of praise songs. White handkerchief-headed ladies, vibrating tambourines in hand, strutted the glory walk up and down the aisles. A head-and-knee-bowed deacon began wailing in tongues. The congregation lifted their voices in a torrent of syncopated moans. The hall was crammed full of the dispersed and hangers-on of a drowned and devalorized Newman Quarters. I scanned all the faces, recognized many of the elderly, some childhood friends, and schoolmates. I also noted the missing and unremembered.

The preacher dismissed us with: "Surely your waste, your desolate places and your devastated land—surely now will be too narrow for your inhabitants, and those who swallowed you up will be far away. The children of your bereavement will yet say in your ears: 'The place is too narrow for me; make room for me to dwell in.' Isaiah 49, verse 19-20."

It was hot as hell outside. The kind of weather that could fry an egg on the sidewalk. I had the good fortune, during her

Montreal years, of befriending Mississippi author Elizabeth Spencer. We took long slow walks, licking our ice cream cones as we ambled on the boardwalk encircling the Port of Montreal.

"Whew this heat," she demurely cackled, "but nothing like the August heat in Mississippi," she distinguished.

I now recalled marking a passage in her courageous novel *Fire in the Morning*: "August in Mississippi is different from July. As to heat, it is not a question of degree but of kind. July heat is furious, but in August the heat has killed even itself and lies dead over us."

It was that kind of August heat that clamped my heat-sizzled and perspiring Sunday-best clothing, as I sweated the large reception line on the lawn. Handshaking, hugs, and reminders of how I know you; how good your parents and grandparents were; how you played baseball; how you were at your mother's funeral; what a good boy you were; how you left home. We remember the homeroom class roll call. Lula Wright. Here. Charles Clark. Here. Leonard Spinks. Here. Luvenia Donaldson. Here. Gracie Hawthorne. Here. Billy McDonald. Here. Leroy Burger. Here. James Nelson. Here. Eugene Smith. Here. Clifford Gaston. Here. Fred Anderson.

"He ain't here."

"He is not here," corrected the teacher.

"Yes mam, he ain't here." That's what I said.

"Is he hurt or sick?"

"No mam. He's gone. Didn't you hear? He a freedom rider, now. People saying that he went off with that Bob Moses man."

"Clifford, what do you know about this?"

"Why are you asking me?"

"You two were sidekicks. He wouldn't do anything without his shadow being in the know."

"My mom told me not to be answering any questions about him."

"Oh, he's no longer Fred. It's now 'him.'"

"Yes mam. Him."

"Alright, enough. Open your books and turn to page seventeen," she ordered.

"She would always call on you to read first. But you were gone. We caught wind of some of the things you were doing. There were whispers that Mrs. Ella Gaston got messages from you. We know your dad must be glad that you're home. He never stopped talking about you and neither did we."

"You don't recognize me, do you? I am the boy that got you in trouble. I stole the oranges."

"Michael. I remember you and the ass whipping," I countered.

Mercifully, the greetings and reminisces waned. People were either beginning the walk home or revving their motors. Tomorrow, we would drive to Columbia, Mississippi to visit my brother Robert and family. I had only recently been informed that he had served in Vietnam. The war, other than the American Civil War, had been one of the most divisive episodes in American history. I was unsure as to how our respective choices had impacted our relationship. He had always been my idol. The way he had nurtured and supported mom in her recovery from a debilitating stroke. His stylish dress. I would often, without permission, purloin his outfits and peacock strut among my friends. He would invariably track me down. Embarrassingly demanding that I immediately go home and disrobe. I was on the junior high football team and wanted to join and emulate his glory on the high school team. His teammates treated me as an undeserving wannabe and gently bludgeoned me towards withdrawal. Robert felt otherwise. I was the shameless sibling out to steal his thunder. He mercilessly taunted and pounded me into the turf. I ignominiously surrendered and retreated to my baseball ambitions.

Mary and I arrived at a spacious house surrounded by trees and expansive grounds.

Robert approached. All the girls and I had always been impressed with his full head of frizzy hair. There were now just a few scrawly tufts. Once tall and brawny, he appeared emaciated. He attributed his appearance to the effects of Agent Orange. The chemical defoliant used by American combatants. His wife was more than ebullient in welcoming Mary and me. His children had been obviously schooled on who I was and genuinely welcomed their uncle Fred from Canada.

Robert invited me to accompany him for a walk in the woods. He told me that he was employed as the supervisor of an adolescent correctional center. I was chilled by the description of the mission and his unfettered authority. I would not have wanted to be among the incarcerated in his charge. It was obvious that he was a 'no excuses' stern disciplinarian. He walked, hands in pockets, ahead of me. Turned, and said, in a muted, regretful tone, "I want you to know that you made the right decision. I know how much you emulated and sought to walk in my shoes. But I recognize and applaud your courage and willingness to risk all. I can tell you that myself, and so many others in my regiment, wish that we had chosen otherwise." He wiped away tears. "Let's go eat," he encouraged.

He was once again the enviable Robert. The brother who had arranged my conditional baseball scholarship to Tennessee State College. That insisted and taught me how to fight bullies. Now lessened by his Vietnam War ordeal but bigger than ever. Damn him. We toured the youth correctional center. It was not much to look at. The general disrepair and dankness, personifying the demeanor of the detainees. The appearance of the pristine gymnasium and athletic complex were disconcerting in comparison to the residences of the inmates. The walls of his office were plastered with photographs and newspaper clippings of his high school glory days and Jackson State College. His many trophies pyramided the glassed-in display. "Nothing to write about. Viet Cong prisoners had better facilities," he bemoaned.

Later, he walked us to the car and placed an object in my left front pocket and said: drive carefully.

"What did he give you," asked Mary. It was a small box, beribboned and emblazoned with an American flag. It was a Vietnam War Service Medal. It was a bewildering and unnerving gesture. I came to view it as an allegory that, unlike him and so many others, I had chosen to take the road less traveled by. Or conversely, it could be viewed as a less grandiloquent act—a simple but transferable affirmation that nothing, not even war, would ever divide us. Perhaps.

It was now Tuesday. We arrived to scoop up dad and drive to Akron, Ohio. Mrs. Alberta had prepared box lunches and refreshments. She waved goodbye from the front gate. Back in Akron we luxuriated in family lore. It was wonderful being together with dad and all but one of my sisters. Johnny Mae was long gone. Dad and I took long morning and evening walks. We were pitmasters for the afternoon barbecues. The days galloped by, and the eventuality of the long goodbye was at hand. I hunkered down in the backyard with dad. I still cherish that moment and the only existing photograph of the two of us.

"Well," he mumbled.

"Yes," I replied.

"I can now die happy," he pronounced.

"Not before we do this again. I love you. Take care of yourself and Mrs. Alberta," I commanded.

He stuffed his hands in the pocket of his pants and looked away. I knew he was crying. None of that, I wanted to say. But didn't. I put my arms around him, and we both kept our gaze downward. It was endings such as these that blew out the candles of my South to *home crossing*.

It was a hushed and traffic-congested drive to the Akron Airport. We lingered at the departure gate.

Mary broke the silence. "Fred, I know that you're uncertain about the future. But we would love to have you back home. There is so much to repair."

"I know and I am weighing it all," I said.

"I know you know," she said, and jerked me in for a kiss.

I headed for the departure gate, turned, and mouthed, "I love you all."

The plane lifted and streaked towards Canada. I was not sure how I felt about all of it. The devastation. The newness. It was all too familiar, simple but complicated, near but far.

Mississippi writer, Willie Morris, in one of his memoirs *North Toward Home* addresses the emotional gravity of itching to escape and the hunger to remain connected.

"His claim to home," he wrote, "is deep, but there are too many ghosts. He must absorb without being absorbed." Which *home*? That was the question. Would I eventually choose another destination? South to home? The wheels thundered down the runway and I knew viscerally, with the thudding halt, that going forward Mississippi was '*away*,' and that I would forever be a visitor.

Ernest Hemingway wrote, "Where a man feels at home, outside of where's he born, is where he's meant to go."

Award-winning Canadian writer Esi Edugyan summed up this recognition in her lectures, *Dreaming of Elsewhere: Observations on Home*: "We leave to come back, changed, made new...I do not think home is a place...I believe home is a way of thinking, an idea of belonging, which matters more to us than the thing itself."

I was in good company; at ease considering all that my eyes have seen. That Canada with its values of inclusiveness, though far from perfect, was fertile and sufficient ground to lay my burdens down.

## Take Me to the Water

There was much that happened in the intervening years. Most notably, in 2010 I did make the trip to five African countries. I made the obligatory visit to Elmina Castle and Cape Coast Castle in Ghana. Two of the principal castles referred to as slave castles. The final points of disembarkment before slaves were loaded onto ships to cross the Atlantic Ocean. Never to return. Crawling through the minuscule slaves' pens was horrifyingly claustrophobic. I stood, peering out The Door of No Return. A narrow opening that led to the water's edge and the waiting slave ships. I struggled to hold back my tears. I would, years later, recall this moment, while reading Canadian author Lawrence Hill's *The Book of Negroes*.

The protagonist, Aminata Diallo, had made this same journey. Her warning now rang with ghostly horror and immediacy: "Let me begin with a caveat to all who find these pages. Do not trust large bodies of water, and do not cross them. If you, Dear Reader, have an African hue and find yourself led toward water with vanishing shores, seize your freedom by any means necessary."

"There, right underneath, lies a bottomless graveyard of children, mothers, and men. I shudder to imagine all the Africans rocking in the deep...."

I continued my watery ways to Cotonou, Benin, to visit the water village of Ganvie, Africa's largest water village of roughly 45,000 stands on stilts in the middle of Lake Nokouve.

The Portuguese slave trade was booming in the seventeenth century. The Tofino tribe, pursued by the slavers of the Fon tribe, fled to Lake Nokouve to avoid being captured and sold to the Portuguese slavers. Legend has it that the fearsome Fon warriors believed that the waters were alive with demon spirits. Their religious beliefs precluded their being near or in water. The sacred lake, on the lagoon, became the safe harbor of the Tofino tribe. They named the water village *Ganvie*, which in their local language means "we survived."

I was invited into the special compound for a renaming ceremony. The Elder bowed, placed her hand atop my head, slowly poured sacred water and declared, "You are now called *Gwissai*, meaning 'he who does not fall down.'"

How is all that for trickster energy?

However, all such subsequent tales are for later telling. Perhaps. "It is not necessary to tell all you know," wrote Harper Lee. Much is forgotten. But I will always remember those that sustained me. Those still standing and I will forever hear the echoing voices of the fallen. Chief among them: Herman Carter and Bob Moses. The irradicable sodality of our journey.

"It stays with me, a bruise in the memory that hurts when I touch it," wrote Jesmyn Ward.

### Above the Tree Line

> *"I think I'm the first man to sit on top of the world. It'll work. If God. wind, leads, ice, snow, and all the hells of this dammed frozen land are willing"*
>
> —Matthew Henson, 1912

I had read Matthew Henson's, *A Negro Explorer at the North Pole, 1912*. Robert Perry (1856–1920) is celebrated as the first explorer to reach the geographical North Pole with one notable erasure. African American explorer, Matthew Henson (1866–1955), had accompanied him on the expedition. Henson was fluent in the local language (Inuktitut). His capacity to translate directions and gather environmental resources proved indispensable. Henson was also proficient in the skills of professional dogsledding, managing crews in icy waters, and

Fred in Inukjuak, December 2017.
(Photo courtesy an Inuk adolescent girl)

employing the survival skills needed for nighttime sheltering. All vitally important for the success of the expeditioners. Perry garnered singular recognition for this milestone accomplishment. Henson was posthumously awarded the National Geographic Society's Hubbard Medal. Almost a century after Perry had been awarded the same honor in 1909.

Here am I, one-hundred and eight years or so later, on the treeless tundra of Inukjuak (December 2017). A small Inuit village, of 1,821, situated in the arctic and subarctic climate zones on Hudson Bay, in the mouth of the Innuksuak River, in Nunavik. It is not accessible by road, but by boat in the summer and year-round by air through Inukjuak Airport.

I was employed by the Nunavik Regional Board of Health and Social Services as Program Manager responsible for Ulluriaq Girls Adolescent Rehabilitation Centre and Kuujjuarapik (co-ed) Teen Group Home. Kuujjuarapik, population 792, is located at the mouth of the Great Whale River. Situated in the southernmost village of Nunavik. The village has the distinction of an Inuit and Cree population. I quickly learned that Inuktitut has one basic word for 'black'—*girnitaq*—as to be black or dark as in blue fox, etc. *Qallunaat* (pronounced "halunat") is an inclusive term for white people. The term, moreover, refers to a state of mind, rather than skin tone. Encompassing all people originating from Canada's southern regions.

It is New Year's Eve day, December 31, 2017. Early tomorrow the sled dogs will be harnessed for an expedition on the land. An Inuit tradition of cultural retention. It is paramount that most, if not all, Inuit youth observe this annual custom. Especially our girls—sequestered by court ordered protection—from physical/sexual abuse, drugs and alcohol use, suicidal ideation and attempts. The perfidious outcome of intergenerational trauma resulting from forced resettlements, horrors of residential schools, and other post-colonial reverberations. Returning to the land is one of the prime means of their remaining familiar with the primordial tenets of traditional knowledge and Inuit way of living. We will be shepherded by our Inuit staffers, a village elder, and a renowned village musher.

The emergency skidoo is already packed with provisions, health kit, emergency heaters, cooking utensils, knives, walkie talkies, and rifle. No telling what lay ahead. A gloriously white polar bear, days ago, had wandered into the village, in search of food. It had been dispatched by members of the Inuit Canadian Rangers contingency and transferred for slaughter and stored in the *"piruliaqs"*—freezers. We could hear, at breakfast light, the yelping of the dogs. The dogs were belted to the *qamutiik*—traditional Inuit sled—in a fan shape using sealskin lines and harness. The six-dog team was arranged into three pairs. The nearest to the sled are the wheel-dogs—the middle huskies are the team dogs—the front two are the leaders. The wheel-dogs, usually males, tend to be larger, and provide the power.

We were off. Hours and miles across the limitless, flat and expansive horizon. An eerie quietude except for the murmur of white noise, yowling-panting dogs, and the croaky sound of sled runners rising and falling over the frozen carpet of snow and ice. The crystalized snow drifts and savage ice pellets burning your eyes, ricocheting off your skin, and inflating your lungs with every breath. I was fiercely and inhospitably cold. The temperature was -28.3 °C. I feared how much further we would journey. The dogs deftly angled leftwards in the opposite direction. As if the musher had divined my uneasiness. The sun had collapsed. The ice and entire landscape was a subdued shimmering sheen. Almost a complete loss of shadow and horizon definition. A plenitude of distant stars, and sliver of moon, our lone source of light. Casting an anemic and dwindling silhouette of sled and dogs. N. Scott Momaday wrote: "It's a landscape that has to be seen to be believed. And, as I say on occasion, it may have to be believed in order to be seen." The musher assured me that lead dogs (called *Isuraqtujuq* in Inuktitut) were trained to get home, even in the most hazardously blinding snowstorm.

We continued inward bound. The dogs yowling and venting frothy steam from mouth and nostrils. We heard, across the interspaces, the treble rejoinder of yapping dogs. We could now barely discern, through the halo of swirling snow, the glistering lights of Inukjuak. A small number of village elders cheering our safe return. The elders gifted me a caribou shoulder. It had been buried in an outdoor stone

Bob Moses and Fred at the Fiftieth Anniversary Reunion of Mississippi Freedom Summer at Tougaloo State College, Jackson, Mississippi, July 2014. (Photo courtesy of James Donald)

Herman Carter. (Photo courtesy of the Carter Family)

pile for nearly a month, defrosted, and stewed with mixed vegetables. It was a one-of-a-kind experience of Inuit culinary traditions. I showered and went to bed underneath the covers of thawing and ineffable dreams.

My cell phone chimed in the early morning hours of January 21, 2018. The email alert, with attached obituary, was from Lance Evoy. Herman Carter was dead. Stupefying news. I had only briefly known Herman prior to our decision to twin our exile to Canada with that of Bob Moses. Herman had been an organizer with the Congress of Racial Equality (CORE). Strategic planning for the Mississippi Summer Project had assigned Mississippi territorial responsibilities between the major civil rights organizations. CORE and SNCC staff rarely crossed paths. Something, nevertheless, sparked an affinity between us. It was our jittery border crossing and the aftermath that cemented our bonds. We had arrived one month before Bob. We had, during the interval, begun to appreciate each other's family histories, sense of humor, and affection for books, sports, jazz, blues, good food, and the nightlife. Herman devoted the past thirty-years to teaching at Dawson College. Expounding on Third World politics, black theatre, and English composition. And now it has come to this. Memories collide. Late nights at the Black Bottom. Stumbling homewards, pissing into the swirling snow, frigid winds, and singing freedom songs. Besotted sessions at the Canadian Legion on Lusignan Street and the comradery of black veterans. Our longings for home and the seminal departure of Bob. And now this baneful finality. I did not attend the funeral. My direct Air Inuit flight from Kuujjuaq to Montreal was grounded due to successive days of blinding blizzard conditions. Our last supper had been at Da Vinci Restaurant on Ste. Catherine Street. Joyous as ever. I recalled all of our previous breaking bread repasts and the words of Native American poet Joy Harjo: "Perhaps the world will end at the kitchen table, while we are laughing and crying, eating the last sweet bite." I decided, at year's end, that it was time to go home. Farewell Inukjuak. The scene of appalling heartbreaks, the abiding and shining bedrock of Inuit cultural resiliency. Goodbye to my reveries of Matthew Henson.

Aboard the Inuit jet, I observed a constellation of radiant stars and remembered the wisdom of an Inuk elder: "Stars are holes in heaven. And every time we see the people we loved shining through, we know they're happy." It is only recently, counterintuitively, that I recognize that I unendingly grieve Herman's death. Subconsciously, and equally revelatory, is the realization that I mourn for myself and his absence in the uninterruptedness of my daily keepings. It was a sombre flight. The words of two of my favorite poets occupying my beleaguered thoughts. Gwendolyn Brooks' "We are each other's harvest; each other's business; we are each other's magnitude and bond," and T.S. Eliot's "We shall not cease from exploration, and the end of all our exploring will be to arrive where we started and know the place for the first time." *Vale, donec nos conveniamus* (until I see you again), Herman.

END

# EPILOGUE

*"Time moves slowly but passes quickly."*
—Alice Walker, *The Color Purple* (1982)

### September 24, 2021

Just disembarked at Boston's Logan International Airport. The memorial service for Bob Moses is tomorrow and will take place in Cambridge, Massachusetts. I was crestfallen but not surprised to receive the phone call—July 25, 2021—informing me of his death. He was sickly and had already rebounded from several near-death experiences. Weeks prior, a video link had been arranged for colleagues to express encouragement and well wishes. Word came that he was on the mend followed weeks later by the fateful call.

A few of us mournful veterans of SNCC assembled in a private lounge at the Godfrey Hotel. Long gone were the stiff-backed days. Each of us now several degrees recurved. Modified gaits. Walkers or walking canes. Distracting tremors. Tremulous but eyes nevertheless still on the prize. Attenuated gladiators. Here to salute the fallen. Choreographed masqueraders. Arm's length, elbow greetings. Still flattening the curve. We huddled in a head-bowed equally spaced circle and hummed the timeless gospel: *"This may be the last time... May be the last time children I don't know..."*

We climbed into a taxi for the drive to Cambridge. All the way singing Sweet Honey and the Rock—*"They are falling all around me... the strongest leaves of my tree..."*

St. Mary of the Annunciation Church crowns the central square of downtown Cambridge. The assembly was by invitation and Covid-sized. Center stage stood a flower draped photograph of Bob, preternaturally camera-shy and averse to adulation. I pondered what he would make of all this. Bob was all about shining the light on others. The order of service and the presenters, save one, spoke about how he had inspired and lifted them up. Each of us to differing degrees sat alone with our thoughts. I bowed my head and genuflected my gratitude for having known him and having walked in his shadow up and down the dusty roads of Mississippi. In search of the crossroad of *One Man, One Vote and Freedom Now.*

I followed the New Orleans-inspired second-line jazz band out the church door into the central square. Jumping and gyrating my hallelujahs for his many gifts. Always the *Mwalimu*—the teacher. All the lessons on the necessity and urgency of asking the right questions; the potency of silence; radical equations and the mathematics of continuous change. Our crossing to Canada and journey's end. *Good traveling, my friend.*

I boarded the flight for Canada. Remembering that we three Vietnam War resisters had chosen exile in Canada: Bob, Herman, and Fred. Now bereft, minus two—alone to bear witness—sole storyteller of the algebraic expression of our passage. I was thinking how to sum up the boil and glow of your life; my sense of loss and what you meant to me and so many. Maya Angelou came to mind "When Great Trees Fall":

"...Our senses, restored, never
to be the same, whisper to us.
They existed. They existed.
We can be. Be and be
better. For they existed...."

# ACKNOWLEDGEMENTS

Lance & Ann Evoy, Wendy & Patrick Quarry, & *J*. Some names have been changed and others must remain nameless. Their steadfast friendship, love, courage, and risk-taking sustained my exile in Canada.

Much appreciation to Wendy and Lance for encouragement and countless hours of proofreading and to Chloe Stuart-Ulin for her transcribing and uber-patience with my many drafts and Steve Roter and Claude Bélanger for photographic assistance. Much appreciation to Aly Ndiaye (a.k.a.) Webster and to Anne Marie Marko for her careful proofreading.

I, alone, am responsible for all misrememberings and all such errors.

I sincerely regret due to low quality photos that my brothers Robert Anderson, Herbert Anderson, Jr. (deceased), and sister Johnnie Mae Anderson (deceased) are not pictorially represented.

### Homage

Bernard Mergler, L'avocat: 1915-1975
Provided pro bono advice and legal assistance over the course of my exile.

### In Memoriam

Herman Carter, September 30, 1943 - January 21, 2018
Robert P. Moses, January 23, 1935 - July 25, 2021

## ALSO FROM BARAKA BOOKS

A JEW IN RAMALLAH AND OTHER ESSAYS
Carla Blank

MY THIEVERY OF THE PEOPLE, STORIES
Leila Marshy

EINSTEIN ON ISRAEL AND ZIONISM, NEW ENRICHED EDIITION
Fred Jerome

CANADA'S LONG FIGHT AGAINST DEMOCRACY
Yves Engler

BLINDED BY THE BRASS RING
Patricia Scarlett

THE SEVEN NATIONS OF CANADA
Solidarity, Vision, and Independence in the St. Lawrence Valley
1660-1860
Jean-Pierre Sawaya

EXILE BLUES
Douglas Gary Freeman

WHY NO CONFEDERATE STATUES IN MEXICO
Ishmael Reed

Printed by Imprimerie Gauvin
Gatineau, Québec